TEARS & TRIBUTES

by
"ZAKIR"

Contents

Introduction 1
Preface 11

1. The Betrayal in Kufa 13
2. Fifty-four Friends 28
3. Akbar, the Hashimite Prince 49
4. The Youths in Karbala 65
5. Abbas — the Standard-Bearer of Husain 83
6. From Cradle to the Grave 91
7. The Supreme Sacrifice 100
8. The Night of Tragedy 127
9. The Captives' Caravan 140
10. The Death in Prison 167
11. Ordeals in Damascus 172
12. Journey's End 194

INTRODUCTION

Sheikh Sadooq, a famous Shia scholar, reports in his famous work *Al-Amali* on the birth of Imam Husein as under:

The neighbour of Umme Ayman reported to the Prophet of Islam that she had been crying throughout the small hours of the previous night. The Prophet sent for her and inquired about the reason for her distress. She said she had seen an upsetting dream. She dreamt that a piece of flesh had fallen apart from the Prophet's body and had descended in her house. 'Do not be unsettled,' said the Prophet, 'A son will be born of my daughter Fatima (a.s.) and you will be his nurse. No doubt, Husein is my part.'[1]

Husein, son of Ali Ibn Abi Talib and Fatima, daughter of the Prophet of Islam, was born in Medina on Thursday, the third of Shabaan, in 3 A.H.[2]

The Prophet named him Husein, whispered Azan in his right ear, Iqamah in his left. On the seventh day, the Prophet got the child's head shaved (*Aqeeqah*) and slaughtered a sheep. Then he told Fatima to weigh the hair and give away equivalent weight of silver in alms. "And give the leg part of the sheep to the nurse," he ordered.[3]

Ibn Sa'ad in his Tabaqat has observed that the names Hassan and Husein were unknown in the pre-lslamic days. He reports this tradition from the Prophet, "The names Hassan and Husein belong to the people of Paradise. The

---

1 See also *Nasikhut Tawareekh*.
2 Majlisi.
3 Badakhshi (*Nuzulul Abrar*).

Arabs in pre-Islamic era did not keep these names."⁴

It must be noted, morever, that the names Muhammad and Ali were also unknown before the advent of Islam.

Husein very much resembled his grandfather, the Prophet, in appearance. "You resemble my father O little one, and not your father," Fatima used to say lovingly. He was put to the care of his grandmother, Umme Salma, whose love and affection for Husein is well-known. She lived long enough to witness Husein depart from Medina for Iraq, and to hear the sad tidings of his martyrdom. Husein was loved by all, just as any younger member of a family would be. Some historians, from the various incidents reported about the affection and love shown by the Prophet for Husein, have concluded that he preferred Husein to Hassan. This is not true. In fact, Hassan and Husein have been mentioned together in all relevant traditions.

These reports of the Prophet's abounding love for the children of Fatima may be considered a natural parental instinct. However, since the Prophet was held in high esteem by his Companions, and every act and word of his was regarded with absolute reverence, the care and tenderness lavished upon Hassan and Husein was taken as a hint that the Prophet wanted them also to love and respect the children. In fact, the Prophet made this explicit everytime.

Once when the Prophet was speaking to the believers, the little boys appeared in their red attire. Approaching their grandfather, they stumbled and fell. The Prophet came

---

4 *Tabaqat al-Kubra.*

down from the pulpit, lifted them up and said, "God has truly said that your wealth and children are a test. I saw these little ones stumble and fall, and my patience was lost."[5]

On another occasion, the Prophet said, "O Allah, I love them both, and so do You. O Allah, bless those who love them with Your mercy." Abdullah Ibn Masoud says that once while the Prophet was prostrating in his prayers, the two little boys playfully sat on his back. The Companions tried to prevent them. After the prayers, the Prophet said, "Leave them, my father be for them and my mother, he who loves me, loves them both."[6]

Husein's childhood coincides with the heyday of Islam. The period of intensified persecution in Mecca was over, and now Muslims were in full vigour and activity. The people of Medina had extended a warm reception to the Prophet and his mission, and they stood by him faithfully. Beset with a situation which was at times cordial and peaceful, and at times subjected to uprisings, opposition and intrusion from Meccans, Husein observed how his father and grandfather were painstakingly fighting to protect and preserve the Word of Allah. He knew of the day when a peace treaty was signed, and of the day when finally Mecca was conquered. That Husein observed and understood all these developments, identified himself with the personality of his grandfather in all spheres, is very much evidenced by his statements and conduct in the later part of his life.

Perhaps the most memorable event of his childhood is

---

5 Ibnu Majah.
6 Imam Nisa'i and Daylami.

his participation in Mubahila. This was in 10 A.H. when he was only seven. A deputation of Sixty Christians of Najran came to the Prophet to discuss the personality of Jesus. The Holy Prophet told them not to deify Jesus as God or His son, for he was only a mortal. The Christians asked the Prophet to name the father of Jesus, thereby suggesting that since Jesus was born of Virgin Mary, the Prophet would helplessly accept God Himself as being the father of Jesus. In reply to this, the following verse was revealed

> Verily, similitude of Jesus with God is as the similitude of Adam; He created him out of dust then said He unto him Be, and he became.

The Christians had no answer to this, but they refused to concede. The Prophet then called them to Mubahila, which means a spiritual confrontation where each side invokes the curse of God upon the liar. The Christians agreed to this.

A shelter was erected on an open place, and the Prophet proceeded with Hassan and Husein by his sides, Fatima immediately behind him, followed by Ali Ibn Abi Talib. The Christians appeared with their holy men, women and children. At the appointed hour, the headmonk of the Christians exclaimed, "By God I see the faces which are capable of moving mountains, if they are raised in prayers." He beseeched the Prophet to abandon the idea of Mubahila, and requested him to allow the Christians to follow their faith against payment of *Jaziya*, a Proptection Tax. One can imagine the impact of this unique triumph of Islam on the tender mind of Husein.

This event took place in the 10th year after Hijra, a year before the Prophet died. There were many Companions around, and the Muslim Society had by now been fully organised. The selection of his own inmates alone for a confrontation of so great consequence has a noteworthy implication. The seriousness and solemnity of the occasion demanded absolute purity. Husein, therefore, is one of the five pure ones, accepted by all Muslim scholars and jurists.

The Prophet died in 11 A.H., when Hassan and Husein had not even completed their first decade of life. Ninety-five days later, they were bereaved of their mother, Fatima. Fate had now entrusted them to the sole care of their father Ali Ibn Abi Talib, a matchless hero of Islam.

Friends and dissenters alike exalted him above all his contempories, in his wisdom, virtue, probity, maturity, knowledge and bravery. "I am one of the slaves of Muhammad," said Ali, thus drawing a fine line between his rank and that of the Prophet, who was decidedly his master and superior.

Soon after the Prophet's death, there was an upheaval in Medina, and the tide steadily turned against the Ahlul Bait, the inmates of the Prophet. For the ensuing 24 years, Ali lived in Medina as a recluse, serving as a counsel to the cause of Islam whenever called upon to do so. Husain grew up under his father's care as a pious, just and virile young man, respected and loved by one and sundry. However, his heart was rent apart when he saw how the teachings of Islam were being abandoned or ignored, and how its grip was being methodically slackened. He studied the designs of the hidden enemies, who under the guise and mantle of Islam, were now openly and unscrupulously working to undermine the very root of Sheriah.

Fatima, the Prophet's daughter, was denied her legacy, the garden of Fidak. All atrocities against the pious Muslims were being condoned, and there was a special preference for relatives and friends. The House of Wealth of the Muslims was emptied on those who deserved the least, only because of their status and influence. This gained momentum in the early days of Caliphates, and reached a climax during the reign of Uthman, who was killed by the aggrieved Muslims. Ali was then requested to take over in 35 A.H., amidst many enemies who aspired to the seat.

Ali set out immediately for a reform; a return to the laws of Islam. The major problems confronting him were the existence of a corrupt and imcompetent administration, unjust social privileges, and a widening gap between the rich and the poor. In his stern measure to undo the mischief of the preceding rules, he dismissed all the governors, and replaced them with men of virtue and probity, like Ibnu Hunayf, and others. The extravagent gifts lavished upon the privileged were returned to the Treasury, and all preferences were withdrawn.

The periods of four years and nine months during which Ali strived to establish the Divine Rule is fraught with wars, dissents and strife. The privileged who were gradually being stripped of their authority and status, rallied together to fight Ali. The battles of Jamal and Siffeen were fought; the Khawarij dissented and came out openly against Ali at Naharwan. The new administration was shaken. Finally, Aii was killed in 40 A.H. while in prayers in the Mosque of Kufa.

Husein's elder brother Hassan was not given the support

by Muslims. They deserted him when Moawiya, the Governor of Syria proclaimed his kingdom by sheer force. Yakubi in his history reports that Hassan made peace with Moawiya, and entering the pulpit and after praising God, he said,

"O people, surely it was God who led you by the first of us, and who has spared your bloodshed by the last of us. I have made peace with Moawiya, and *I know not whether haply this be not for your trial, and that ye may enjoy yourselves for a time.* (Qur'an)." Thus he preserved the lives, property, and families of his followers from the aggression of Moawiya and his companions. The Imamat of Hassan continued the same way as the Imamat of Ali during the times of three Caliphs, for this was by divine appointments which could not be divested.

Husein witnessed all these uprisings, steadily preparing to face what destiny had in store for him. Moawiya's rule continued for more than a decade, and now the seat of Caliphate was openly converted to that of an earthly kingdom. There was a Court, and a group of bodyguards for the King, who was not easily accessible. Pomp and grandeur replaced the Islamic simplicity, and it soon became a far cry to the days of the Prophet. In 50 A.H. Hassan, despite his resignation, was poisoned and killed. Moawiya during his lifetime, appointed Yazid as his successor. There was an opposition in Hejaz against this unprecedented move, but Moawiya managed to subdue it by threats and cajole.

Husain was still being recognised by Muslims in Hejaz and Kufa as a stalwart of Islam. People referred to him in all their difficulties, sought his advice for their problems. The household of the Prophet maintained its reputation for piety, knowledge and charity. Marwan, a faithful lieutenant of the Omayyids, wrote to Moawiya describing the situation with much anxiety, "Omar Ibn Osman has informed me that a group of Iraqis and some leaders of Hejaz frequent at Husein's place. He has shown some anxiety over these visits, and believes that they might be planning for an uprising. I have carried out some investigations, and am satisfied that Husein has no desire to attempt the empire. However, Husein is a potential danger to your successor. Let me know your opinion."[7]

This letter terribly disturbed Moawiya, and he decided to contact Husein directly, inquiring about the truth in the information conveyed by Marwan.

Husein made a lengthy reply to Moawiya assuring him that he was not planning for any surge. However, Husein made following remarks which Moawiya obviously did not like. He wrote:
"O Moawiya, the news given to you does not have any element of truth. It is an allegation against me by some of your friends and flatterers. You know very well that I do not intend to wage a war against you, though, By God, I do not like to leave you unchallenged after the atrocities you have committed against the pious men like Hujr bin Adi, Amru bin Humuq, Alkhizai and others."

Muir in his *Annals of the Early Caliphate*, says that Moawiya, on his death bed, cautioned Yezid: "As for al-Husein, the restless men of Iraq will give him no peace till he attempt the empire; but when thou has gotten the victory, deal gently with him, for truly the blood of the Prophet runneth in his veins." It is difficult to accept this

---

7 Belgrami - *Zibhe Azeem*.

report as true because Moawiya is well-known for his adverse attitude to Ali and his sons. Upon the receipt of Husein's letter, Moawiya retorted to Husein, "You are a fat sheep, whose blood is bubbling for a butcher's knife." The words of caution to Yezid was, therefore, a calculated and disguised expression of a wish, which Yezid understood and fulfilled.

When Yezid ascended his father's throne, he demanded homage and allegience from Husein. He was rebuffed by the words which have been noted down by all the historians, "A person like me would never give allegience to a person like him," Husein said.

Upon death of Moawiya, Yezid was proclaimed an absolute monarch in Damascus in 60 A.H. After the burial, he came to the Green Dome built by his father and read a long euology for his father enumerating his achievements. The Treasury was then opened, and gifts were generously distributed among the leaders of the tribes and clans.[8]

Yezid was known for his indulgence and corrupt practices. He was drunkard, committing adultery and making a mockery of Sheriat. He is reported to have declared, "The family of Hasham has staged a play to acquire kingdom. Actually, there was never an angel nor was there a revelation." This sums up his character as well as his belief.

Acting on his father's advice, Yezid wrote to his governor at Medina to secure recognition and allegiance from Husein. Husein declined, and left Medina for Mecca on the

---

8 *A'sam Koofi.*

28th of Rajab, 60 A.H. He was accompanied by his family, and a handful of near relatives. While in Mecca, Husein continued receiving letters from Kufa inviting him to go there. On the 15th of Ramadhan same year, he sent his cousin Muslim Ibn Aqeel to Kufa as his emissary. While Yezid sent Ibnu Ziyad to Kufa to prevent Muslims from gaining a hold there, he also sent some spies in the guise of Hajis to Mecca with a commission to kill him even in Haram of Ka'aba. Husein left Mecca when the Haj days were well nigh and proceeded to Iraq.

The following pages, written by "ZAKIR," give a detailed treatment to the tragedy of Kerbala, where Husein and his handful of companions were mercilessly slain.

This Edition is the third and revised edition and we are grateful to the Author for permission to revise and re-print the book. We are also grateful to Mr. George Spence of Mombasa for editing it.

Asgharali M. M. Jaffer,
Chairman,
Bilal Muslim Mission of Kenya

Preface

The new moon of the month of Muharram heralds the New Year of the Islamic calendar. It is customary for all nations to celebrate their New Year with feasting and rejoicing but, in contrast, all Islamic countries, instead of celebrating their New Year with revelries and merry-making, go into morning. The New Year is not ushered in with the ringing of bells, display of flags and buntings and dances of belles but by singing of dirges and beating of breasts. A person who is not familiar with Islam and its chequered history, is at times puzzled and perlexed at what he beholds and, out of curiosity, asks for the reasons for the heart-rending scenes he sees. When he is told that the mourning is for the martyrs of Karbala, who laid down their lives for the cause of truth, more than thirteen hundred years ago, he naturally wants to know who the martyrs were and how their sacrifices and sufferings evoke such emotions and stir the hearts of Muslims in spite of the lapse of centuries.

The history of mankind is replete with instances of great souls and saintly persons laying down their lives for the sake of ideals they cherished, for the sake of causes they espoused, for principles they upheld. Such noble examples arc recalled and remembered but very seldom mourned like the tragedy of Karbala. To understand the real significance of this great carnage and its impact on Islamic history, it is necessary to study the annals of Islam from its inception. What led Imam Husain, the grandson of Prophet Muhammad (Peace be on him) to sacrifice his all for the sake of truth and the principles of Islam, and what was the cause he was defending, can be understood only by an unbiased and dispassionate study of the chronicles of those times. Then only it can be appreciated that it was not a family feud culminating in a massacre but a fight by Imam Husain, son of Maula Ali, and grandson of the Prophet (Peace be on him), and his devoted followers, who suffered untold hardships and laid down their lives for the sake of principles inculcated by Islam, for the defence of ideals which they considered far more precious than their lives. It was not a conflict and fight for a kingdom or for dominance but for the defence of principles, for demonstration to all mankind, for all time, that might is not right; to establish beyond doubt that sufferings and martyrdom are essential when the cause is just; to prove that the victor and the vanquished cannot be determined by the immediate results of a battle or war but by the long-term repercussions of the clash of their ideologies on the course of events and influence on the minds of men.

The happenings on that fateful 10th day of Muharram of 61 A.H. and their aftermath were so soul-stirring that they have left an indelible impression on the minds of millions of Muslims who recall them with the deepest feelings and emotions. The sufferings of Imam Husain and those with him, who participated in those events, defy description and it is not possible to do justice to the theme. This is just a brief attempt at recollection of the events of the day and the happenings thereafter. If the interest of those who read it is aroused to find out for themselves, by reference to the history of Islam, the causes that led to the sacrifice, the purpose will be achieved. To others who know the significance of the martyrdom of Imam Husain, and its impact on the course of Islamic history, this work will appear as what it is intended to be—a tribute in tears.

The Betrayal in Kufa

Pin-drop silence prevailed in the mosque at Kufa where a large congregarion had gathered to offer evening prayers. Outside the mosque the town-crier was reading out the proclamation. Every one of the congregation was straining his ears to listen to every word with rapt attention.

At the top of his voice the town-crier was shouting: "Be it knowrjlo the people of Kufa that Obeidullah, son of Ziad, has assumed the governorship of Kufa under the orders of the Khalif. He has noted with perturbation that the people of Kufa have extended their welcome to Muslim, son of Aqil, who has come from Medina as an emissary of Husain, son of Ali, who has declined ro owe allegiance to the Khalif. It is hereby proclaimed for the information of all the citizens of Kufa that any person found associating with Muslim, son of Aqil, will be considered a rebel against the Khalif and, by way of punishment, he will be hanged, drawn and quartered, his entire family will be put to the sword and his property confiscated. In case of those who have hitherto extended their welcome to him, if they now repent and desist from doing so, amnesty will be given."

With bated breath every one listened to the proclamation. It was this same Muslim, son of Aqil, who was to lead the prayers that evening, and as the proclamation ended, he rose to fulfil his duty. A few exchanged enquiring glances with their friends. Some others whispered some words to their neighbours. At this moment the call for prayers was given and Muslim silently rose to lead the congregational prayers.

When Muslim completed the prayers and turned back the found the mosque empty, except for one person only — Hanee Ibne Orwah at whose house Muslim was staying as a guest. The two looked at each other. No words were needed to tell Muslim why the people of Kufa had deserted him. The people of Kufa, who had so persistently asked Husain to come over to them and take up the responsibilities of their spiritual amelioration had, on hearing the proclamation, got scared out of their wits. These were the people who had in the past betrayed Muslim's uncle Ali, the Commander of the Faithful, and shown cowardice in times of trouble and tribulations. These were the people who had deserted Muslim's cousin, Hasan, son of Ali, in his hour of need.

Muslim stood for a while motionless. His face was full of anguish. He was not dismayed at the fate that awaited him, because a fighting death was the heritage of his family. He was only disconsolate at the thought that he had reposed confidence in these people's sincerity and written to his cousin, Husain, to come over to Kufa as their moral, mental and spiritual preceptor, to save them from sinking into the depths of moral degradation. How he wished he had not been hasty about judging these people!

A moment's reflection was sufficient to make up his mind. At least there was one man with him who could be relied upon by him. If he could only send a message to Husain through Hanee Ibne Orwah about the treachery of the people of Kufa! If he could send a warning to Husain about the betrayal and make him change his course!

With these thoughts Muslim turned towards Hanee.

Before he could give expression to his thoughts, Hanee Ibne Orwah anticipated his words. In low whispers he said: "Muslim, my respected guest, I know what is uppermost in your mind. If God enables me to leave this cursed town in time, I shall rush post-haste to warn our master and Imam to turn back." He hung his head down and, in a tone which was hardly audible, added, as if muttering to himself: "Muslim, my duty towards you as your host demands that I should remain here to protect you and shed the last drop of my blood in your defence. Bur I know that you would like me to attend to the higher duty which we both owe to our Lord, Husain Ibne Ali. There is hardly any time to be lost and so I bid you farewell. May Almighty God protect you and your innocent sons from the fury of these treacherous fiends."

Hanee Ibne Orwah rushed out of the Mosque. He knew that he had to act quickly, if at all he was to succeed in his mission. Before leaving Kufa he had to do something for the safety of the two young sons of Muslim who had not yet reached their teens. He was quickly revolving in his mind how he could hide these innocent boys and where. He could not think of anybody known to him who could be trusted to give shelter to them. He hardly had any time at his disposal to make arrangements because his paramount obligation was to convey Muslim's message to Imam Husain. His quick-working mind decided that the children of Muslim may be warned to get out of the house where they were no longer safe and leave the rest to God.

On reaching his house, Hanee asked his wife to whisk the children out of the house by the back dcor for their safety. He asked his servant to harness his horse as quickly as he could. Hardly Muhammad and Ibrahim, the young sons of Muslim, had been put on the road to face the world and its turmoils in a strange and unfriendly city, the house of Hanee was surrounded by armed troupers sent by Obeidullah. Hanee realised that the hope he had cherished to leave the town and carry the message of Muslim to Husain was completely frustrated. He unsheathed his sword and fell upon the hirelings of Obeidullah with the intention of selling his life as dearly as he could. The odds against him were too heavy. He was soon overpowered and chained and marched off to the court of the Governor.

****

After Hanee's departure from the Mosque, Muslim reflected for a while. At first his mind was put at ease by Hanee's assurance that he would carry the warning to Husain about the happenings in Kufa. But on second thought he realised that here was every possibility of Hanee being captured before he could leave the town. What if that happened? He had fullest confidence in Hanee's sincerity, but how could he be so sure that Hanee would be able io make good his escape from Kufa? Although Muslim was fully alive to the lot that would befall his innocent sons on their caputre, he realised that the right course for him was to find some other person whom he could trust to carry the message to the Imam. Kneeling down in prayers he muttered: "Merciful Allah, spare me for a while so that I can send the warning to my Imam."

He came out of the mosque slowly. He did not know which way to turn. He only knew that the whole town had turned hostile to him. As soon as he stepped out of the mosque, he saw groups of people collected hither and thither and engaged in animated conversation. On seeing him coming out they scattered and walked away as if they had never known him. Muslim realised that they were, one and all, mortally afraid of the reprisals that would befall them if they stood by him. Now he saw how difficult it was for him to find a single person who could fulfil his purpose. But where to look for him; where ro find him?

With a heavy heart Muslim was now trudging the narrow by-lanes of Kufa. The sun was fast descending and the dark narrow lanes of Kufa becoming darker every moment. Making a hood of his gown, so as to cover his head ro avoid identification Muslim was walking on and on, almost aimlessly ambling. The deserted cobbled pavements were echoing his foot-steps. The only other sound to be heard was of the horses' hoofs as the soldiers were patrolling the streets and searching for him in all nooks and corners. Whilst walking aimlessly he was furiously thinking how to find someone who could carry his message to Husain.

Soon darkness descended on the whole town. As curfew had been imposed by the orders of the Governor, not a soul was venturing out. It became evident to Muslim that, if he walked on, there was every possibility of his being arrested by the patrolmen and, if that happened, his last hope of finding a messenger would vanish. The events of the day had made him tired in body and soul. He decided to sit on the doorsteps of a house and rest for a while. Perhaps he thought he could ask for a cup of water from some inmate of that house to quench his thirst.

He sat on the doorstep of a house, hesitating whether to knock at the door and ask for water. Whilst he was still wavering, he heard the opening of the door against which he was leaning. An old lady stood before him with a flickering candle in her hands. From her enquiring eyes he could understand that she was wondering why he was seated there. Muslim turned to her and requested her for a glass of water. She asked him to wait for a minute and, going into the house, returned with a tumbler of water. Muslim drank it to the last drop and thanked the lady profusely. He again sat down on the doorstep. The old lady looked at hint for a while and then asked him: "My son, why do you not return to your house? Do you realise how your wife and children must be worrying about you by your remaining away from the house in such troubled atmosphere? Don't you have a house with wife and children?" A lump came into Muslim's throat with the recollection of his family and home. Controlling his emotions and checking the tears which were gushing from his eyes he said: "Good lady, I have a house, but in a distant land. My wife and young daughters are at home and my sons are in Kufa but perhaps they will wait for me forever." After a brief pause he added: "In this unfriendly town I have no home and no soul to whom I can turn for shelter."

These words of despondency moved the lady. Sympathetically she said: "You appear to he a traveller or wayfarer from some distant land. From where do you come and why are you here in these troubled times?"

Muslim murmured in reply: "I am from the city of the Prophet. I came on the invitation of the people of Kufa as their guest. Though thousands welcomed me on my arrival, there is now not a soul who will admit me into his house."

The venerable old lady was taken aback by this reply. She raised the candle she was carrying to bring it nearer Muslim's face. With an exclamation of recognition she bent down on her knees and said: "My God, you are Muslim, the emissary of my Imam, my beloved Husain, who is hunted by Obeidullah's soliders. How did I not recognise you at the first glance when your words, your accent, your demeanour, all had the stamp of people of the Prophet's House." Sobbing bitterly and overcome by contrition she added, "How will I face my lady Fatima on the day of reckoning when she will ask me: 'Taha, my Husain's emissary came to you, friendless and shelterless, but you callously and relentlessly turned him out!' What reply will I give to her? The least that I can do for you is to give you shelter in try house till an opportunity arises for you to make good your escape from this cursed city whose people are steeped in perfidy."

Muslim felt reluctant to accept her offer for fear that the Godfearing old lady might be victimised for giving him protection. But on second thought he decided to stay in her house with the hope that, if he could avoid arrest for some time, he might be able to find some one to carry his message to Husain.

Taha asked Muslim to remain in the attic of the house. She gave him whatever food there was in the house but he could hardly partake of anything. How can a person in his predicament relish food? He decided to pass the night in prayers as if had a premonition that this would be his last night.

Before retiring into the attic, Muslim told Taha about his desire to send a message to the Imam not to come to

Kufa in view of what had transpired. She assured him that when her son, who was in the Government armed forces, returned from his beat, she would take him in her confidence and enlist his support in finding some reliable person for this job.

Hardly a few hours had passed wher Taha's son returned home. He looked tired and worn out. When Taha enquired from him the reason for his coming home so late, he told her that, along with other soliders, he was patrolling the streets in search of Muslim. She was aghast at the thought that her son, of all people, should be in the party searching for Muslim, when she herself was so devoted to the House of the Prophet. She strongly protested to her son at the role he was playing. That cunning man turned round and assured his mother that, though he had in the course of his duty to pretend as if he was searching for Muslim, in reality he was as much devoted to Muslim, and the House of the Prophet, as she was. His disingenuous assurances carried conviction to the simple old lady and, after making him swear by his faith, she took her son into confidence and told him everything about the happenings of that evening. The crafty son of Taha was inwardly elated at the thought that he would be able to collect the prize placed on Muslim's head. His first thought was to behead Muslim in his sleep but, a coward that he was, he got scared at the fate that would befall him if Muslim would wake up before he accomplished his purpose. He thought furiously for a few moments and then decided to go and inform Obeidullah Ibne Ziad that he had Muslim in his house and he could be easily captured. His warped mind quickly invented an excuse for going out in the dead of night, without arousing the suspicions of his noble mother. He told her that, as in his presence, Hanee Ibne

Orwah, at whose house Muslim and his two sons were staying, had been beheaded and as the two young boys were roaming the streets of Kufa, he thought it his bounden duty to search for them and bring them home so that the father and sons could be reunited. He told Taha that he would also see one of his trusted friends and through him arrange to convey Muslim's message to the Imam for which he was so anxious. Taha was taken in by the guiles of her perfidious son. She felt elated that her son was so keen to do the good work that he could not wait till the daybreak.

The avaricious son of Taha hastened to the Governor's house and lost no time in getting himself admitted to his presence. In fact Obeidullah was awake waiting for the news of Muslim's arrest as he was mightily afraid that, if Muslim would remain at large, he might succeed in rallying round him a few persons who could offer very stiff opposition to his forces and even upset his ugly plans. He felt relieved and overjoyed at the tidings brought to him by Taha's treacherous son. He immediately ordered one of the comnnnders of his forces to get together a well-equipped contingent for Muslim's arrest.

Accompanied by mounted soldiers, the traitor returned to his house for Muslim's arrest. Muslim was at that time engaged in prayers. When he heard the beating of several horses' hoofs on the paved roads, he understood that the soldiers had come for his arrest. He snatched his sword wfhich was lying by his side and rushed out. Taha stood at the threshold of her house flabbergasted to see that her son had brought the soldiers for the arrest of her revered guest. She fell on Muslim's feet and cried: "Muslim, my prince, how can I explain to you that I have not betrayed you but my cursed son, whom I trusted and never suspected of such blatant treachery, has ruined me. I shall not let them cross my threshold except over my dead body." Muslim did not require to be told that Taha's averments were sincere. He gently told her, "My benefactor, I know that you Lave been very kind and considerate to me and the thought of selling me out cannot even cross your noble and pious mind. I do not in the least blame you for the treachery of your son. As your guest, who has partaken of your hospitality, I cannot allow you to be killed by these merciless brutes and let your house be reduced to shambles. Let me go out of the house and sell my life as dearly as I can."

Muslim gently pushed aside Taha from the threshold and walked out with sword in his hand. By this time the soldiers had reached the house. They were taken by surprise at seeing Muslim emerging from the door like an enraged lion. The lane was so narrow that two horses could not come up abreast. This gave Muslim the best opportunity for single combat. Though he was on foot and the soldier opposite to him was mounted, he possessed the prowess which was the heritage of Ali's family. One after the other the soldiers were tasting the sword of this warrior and falling down from their horses. In the process they were getting crushed and trampled under the hoofs of horses of their own men.

The leader of the hand of soliders, who had discreetly kept himself behind his men, sent word for more men. Though more and more soldiers were pouring in, the topography of the scene or this street battle was such that they could not attack en-masse. Heads of enemy soldiers were falling like nine-pins. Hours passed but still Muslim was fighting his defensive battle most courageously.

When Obeidullah Ibne Ziad's couriers, who were bringing to him the news of the fight, informed him that Muslim was giving a fight the like of which had not been seen since the days of Ali, the Khalif, he got infuriated. He tauntingly asked his generals how many thousands of warriors they needed to capture one solitary person. One of them angrily retorted to him that he was forgetting that the person to be captured was not an ordinary home-keeping youth or shop-keeper but a renowned warrior of the House of Ali. He even suggested that if Obeidullah had no confidence in the generals, he could himself demonstrate his skill with the sword by offering combat to Muslim. This suggestion scared the wits out of Obeidullah. He, of all people, knew what it meant to cross swords with Ali's nephew. Swallowing the taunt, he replied: "My good general, I fully know what it means to fight with a person so desperate who finds himself at bay. Instead of letting our men die by his sword in such large numbers, why cannot some one adopt some stratagem to make him leave his vantage position so that it may be easier to attack him from ali sides?"

This suggestion appealed very much to the cowardly soldiers of Kufa. After some consultations amongst themselves, they decided to send soldiers to the top of the roof of an adjoining building and from there to hurl stones, burning embers and missiles at Muslim. It did not take them long to carry out their strategy. With showers of arrows, stones, fire and missiles, Muslim was so much wounded that he decided to give up his vantage position. He charged on the soldiers in front of him and they fell back. He went forward, wielding his sword, and in the process, sending those who were within its reach to the perdition and doom which they merited.

Once again hasty counsels were held among the captains of the army. Some one suggested that, since Muslim was now desperately moving forward, a trench could be dug on the road and covered up with straw so that it was completely camouflaged. The idea was to trap Muslim as he marched forward. It was realised that, without such subterfuge, Muslim could not he killed or captured without sacrificing the cream of the army.

The treacherous ruse planned by Obeidullah's mercenaries worked as planned. While rushing on and wielding his sword dexterously, Muslim fell into the trench. Now those who were avoiding to come within the reach of his sword swooped down on him. With gushing blood Muslim could not regain his feet. He toppled over and lay unconscious in the trench. It was now a matter of minutes to capture him and soon he was chained and bound.

When Muslim regained consciousness, he found himself a captive. His wounds had accentuated his thirst. The dawn was now breaking and the call for prayers was raised in the mosques of Kufa. Muslim requested his captors to give him some water to drink and for ablution. Instead of acceding to his request, they mocked amt jeered at him. Muslim was extremely surprised and pained to see that the people of Kufa, who were claiming to be the followers of the Prophet, were flouting the injunctions of Islam for kindness to all in a helpless predicament. Little did Muslim know that these same people would behave with utter callousness and beastliness towards Husain and his children in the not too distant future!

Before being marched off to the Court of Obeidullah,

Muslim was paraded through the streets of Kufa with heavy chains on his hands and feet. The people of Kufa, who only a few days before were vying with one another just to have a glimpse of him, were now watching him from their windows with perfect equanimity, as if he was an utter stranger to them. Some devils amongst them were hard-hearted enough to pelt stones at him.

When Muslim was presented before Obeidullah he stood erect with dignity. The Governor asked him whether he knew the fate that awaited him and his master Husain Ibne Ali. With utter disdain Muslim replied "O mercenary of Yazid, I do not cire what you do to me, but I do not like to hear your cursed tongue mentioning Husain's name."

Oheidullah Ibne Ziad felt crestfallen at this bold rebuke of Muslim. With the intention of creating an impression of his magnanimity on the people who were gathered in his court, he said to Muslim, "According to the age-old Arab custom I want you to mention your last desire before you are beheaded so that I may fulfil it."

A glint of hope came into Muslim's eyes. Could he take this man at his word and ask him to send the message which he wanted to be conveyed to his master? Like a drowning man who catches at a straw, Muslim decided that, if at all, this was his only chance. He immediately replied: "Oheidullah, if you are true to your word, fulfil my last wish and send a message to my master Imam Husain, asking him to go back to Medina and abandon the idea of his visit to Kufa."

Obeidullah had never expected this request from Muslim. He had thought that perhaps Muslim might request him to spare the lives of his two young sons when they were captured, as they were sure to be. For a while he was nonplussed; he was at a loss what to say. He knew that he could not fulfil this wish of Muslim without incurring the displeasure of Yazid; but to decline this request would betray him in his true colour. His crooked mind did nor take long to find a solution to this problem. He beckoned to his executioners to take Muslim to the top of the Government House and to behead him. He immediately dismissed his court and hurried back to his apartment.

When the sword of the executioner was swaying over Muslim's head, his last thoughts were with his master, Husain, whom he had loved and cherished more than anything in life. His only regret was that till the end he could not do what he wanted most, to warn Husain against the treachery of the people of Kufa. As the sword fell on his head he silently muttered a prayer to God to so ordain that Husain may come to know of the happenings in Kufa. This was the last prayer of the brave warrior who stood steadfast in death as in life.

Merciful God did not allow Muslim's last prayer to go in vain. He who listens to the prayers emanating from the hearts of sincere devotees like Muslim, enabled one witness to the ghastly enactments of that day, who had some sparks of faith in him, to go riding out of Kufa at the earliest opportunity. He reached the camp of Imam Husain a few days after Muslim's martyrdom. He conveyed the sad tidings to Husain who wept bitterly as if his heart would rend. He called the young daughter of Muslim, who was travelling with him, and told her that thenceforth she should regard him as her guardian. He gave one pair of earrings to her and one to Sakina. When the messenger asked him whether he was turning back and returning to Medina in view of what had happened to Muslim, he replied: "I am going forward to meet my destiny; to fulfil the purpose of my life. My death is beckoning to me and so there is no question of my retracing my steps."

Fifty Four Friends

Some poet, mentioning about battles has said: "Few, few shall part, where many meet." In a way this is true for most of the battles recorded in history. But the battle of Karbala is unique in one respect. Not a single soldier from Husain's army survived on that fateful day. Husain and his faithful followers were outnumbered to an extent which is almost unimaginable in case of a battle. Still what valour they displayed, what heroic feats they performed, what glorious examples they set to the coming generations!

In other respects too, the battle of Karbala can claim unique features. This was the only battle before the start of which the Commander did not think it necessary to exhort his soldiers to fight bravely or to stick to their ground. On the other hand Husain assembled his devoted followers on the night before the battle and, in a touching address, explained to them that they were free to leave him and go away with their dear ones. "Dear friends and kinsmen," he said, "I know what hardship and privations you have suffered in rallying to my side. Yazid and his men are after my blood and, if you decide to leave me, they will be too happy to give you a safe passage out of Karbala. If you think that I shall consider it a desertion and betrayal in case you leave me now, let me assure you that I consider what you have already done for me to be enough to earn my gratitude and the pleasure of God." He added after some thought, "Perhaps you may be feeling embarrassed to leave me like this. I am, therefore, putting out the lights so that, in the dark, nobody will know who has left me." Saying this, he ordered the lights to be put out. In that dark tent not a soul stirred. The faithful friends and relatives of Husain were too much overcome by their emotions to say anything. After a while, when Husain saw that they would not budge an inch, he lighted the candles again. He saw all his devoted friends and loving kinsmen standing silently with heads bent and tears flowing from their eyes. Some of them were old and bent with age; some of them were young and still in the prime of youth. Others had just reached the threshold of youth. At last, the silence was broken by Habib Ibne Mazahir who spoke on behalf of all the faithful companions: "Husain, to us you are everything. How can we explain to you that for each one of us life would be a meaningless burden without you. It is not only because we know that you are the grandson of the Holy Prophet but also because we know that we cannot find a person like you, so kind, so considerate, so loving and so helpful. Although we cannot dare to call ourselves your friends, because you are so superior to us in every way, still we know that you have always treated us as if we were not what we are, your humble followers, but as if we were your dearest friends." The sentiments expressed by Habib Ibne Mazahir were echoed by all the faithful companions, Muslim Ibne Ausaja, Buraire Hamadani, Zuhair Ibne Kain and others. With one voice they said: "We can only consider ourselves successful in life if we die in defending you. Without you life for us would not he worth a day's purchase." What brave souls were these faithful followers of Husain! What a unique attachment they had for him!

The friends and followers of Husain who had gathered round him in Karbala were from different walks of life, But all of them had some thing in common amongst them — their unflinching devotion for Husain, their undying love and affection for him; their supreme faith in the justice of his cause. Some of them were freemen, soldiers bold and true. Others were bondsmen who had come there with their masters but without any compulsion. Even when their masters granted them freedom and asked them to go away where they liked, not one of them budged an inch; not one of them even for a moment thought of leaving Karbala to save his life. On the contrary they earnestly entreated, out of love which was too deep-rooted and sincere to be described, that they wanted only one thing and that was freedom to lay down their lives in defending Husain. With what simplicity Jawn, the freed slave had asked: "O my lord, I am a negro slave and people say that we black people have black blood also. Give us the privilege of having our blood mingled with the blood of the martyrs on the plains of Karbala to prove that we too have feelings of devotion; that we too can respond to the call of duty without any compulsion with the spontaneity of freemen of the highest order." Overpowered by the exuberance of his emotions, he had supplicated that he should not be denied the right to demonstrate his undying devotion and love for Husain.

On that day, in the face of trials and tribulations Husain had only the consolation of knowing that he had with him a hand of faithful supporters the like of whom the world had not seen. They were persons who relegated all personal considerations to the secondary plane, who did not for a moment think of what would happen to their ladies and children who survived them. The only thought uppermost in their minds was to protect and defend Husain and his family and in doing so, to consider no sacrifice too great.

To persons acquainted with these noble souls it would

not be a matter of surprise that they were displaying such unflinching determination to die fighting for Husain. Was not Habib lbne Mazahir attached to Husain from his childhood with affection unique even for a friend? In Medina, during the lifetime of the Prophet, when Habib was a child of about 8 years and was playing with other lads of his age, the Prophet had picked hint up, whilst parsing by, and had fondly caressed the child. The companions of Muhammad (s.a.), who were with him at that time, were surprised at this because, although they knew his love and affection for children, his picking up this child in particular had seemed inexplicable to them. One of them had ventured to ask Muhammad (s.a.) the reason for this special fonding of this boy Habib. Muhammad (s.a.), with tears in his eyes, had replied that he had seen Habib devotedly following his Husain wherever he went; he had seen him literally kissing the ground treaded by Husain. The Prophet added that he could foresee a day when this very child would befriend Husain in a manner which would make his name immortal. Surely this was the occasion Muhammad (s.a.) was referring to.

Husain must be aware of this prophecy for, when he arrived in Karbala, the first thing he did was to write to Habib, who was in Kufa, informing him that he and his kinsmen had arrived in Karbala and were surrounded by Yazid's hordes. When Habib received this letter, he was having his dinner with his wife. On reading the letter he wept bitterly. When his wife asked him what had happened, he told her about its contents. He also told her that, earlier that day, when he had gone to the market to buy henna, he had heard the news that the forces sent by Obeidullah Ibnc Ziad, Governor of Kufa, to massacre

Husain and his family, had surrounded him from all sides. He told her that, on hearing about this, he had thrown away the henna which he had purchased for dyeing his hair and decided that there would be no need for it now since his own blood, flowing in Husain's defence, would dye his hair. He added that, since that time, he was breeding over how he should break this news to her. He offered to give her freedom and all he had, if she so desired. That faithful lady told Habib that she would stand by him. She said that she was feeling proud at the noble decision that he had taken to lay down his life in defence of Husain. She added: "A friend in need is a friend indeed. You have been taking pride in the fact that Husain treats you and regards you as his childhood friend, his faith in you is borne out by the fact that, of all people, he has written to you in his hour of need. I wish you Godspeed."

Habib was possessed by one thought — to reach Karbala as quickly as possible so that his reaching there may not become too late. Tie asked his faithful slave, whom he had taken in his confidence and informed about his plans, to take his horse outside the town that very night and wait for him there so that he could quietly go there to ride towards Karbala without anybody knowing about it. When in the dead of night Habib reached the spot where his slave was waiting for him with the horse, he heard the slave impatiently muttering: "I wonder what has delayed my master so much. If he has been arrested on his way to this place, or prevented forcibly from coming here, I shall myself ride off to Karbala on this horse and tell Husain that my master was not forgetful of his obligations, was not oblivious of the demands of faithful friendship, but was forcibly prevented from coming. It would be the acme of success in life for me if I can fight for Husain and lay down my life in defending him." Habib blessed his faithful slave for his nobility and freed him on the spot. Leaving Kufa, he reached Karbala on the night of the 9th of Muharram, when Husain was distributing arms amongst the few selfless souls who were left in his camp. He had kept aside one set of arms and, when some of his companions asked him the reason for doing so, he replied: "Habib, my dearest friend, is sure to come when he hears about my plight. These arms arc kept for him."

In Husain's camp there was a young lad, Wahab, who had just got married and was returning to his hometown with his mother and the newly-wed bride. Passing through Karbala, they found some tents pitched on one side and a large army posied against the few in those tents. On enquiries Wahab came to know that Husain, son of Ali, and grandson of the Prophet had been surrounded on all sides by Yazid's hordes who were insisting on Husain either to accept Yazid's spiritual leadership or to die at their hands. Wahab carried the news to his wife and mother. The mother of Wahab, who had known Husain from his childhood and who was an ardent admirer of Ali for his fearless battles against forces of tyranny and oppression, knew that Husain would never yield to these threats and bow his head in submission to the will of a profligate and debauchcrous person like Yazid, who had openly flouted all the injunctions of Islam and who was talcing pride in defying and breaking Islamic principles, precepts and practices. When Moaviya, the father of Yazid, was ruling in Damascus and propagating hatred of Ali and the Prophet's family, this courageous lady, who was living at that time in Damascus, had been openly denouncing the tyranny and sacrilegious practices of

Moaviya. As was Moaviya's practice, he had tried to win over this bold lady of influence by offering her large sums of money in return for her agreeing to stop praising Ali and acknowledging allegiance to him. She had, with unmitigated contempt, spurned this offer to Moaviya's amazement and chagrin. In surprise Moaviya had asked her how she could be so adamant when she knew that Ali would not give her even a silver Dirham whereas he was offering her a large sum in solid gold coins. With characteristic frankness she had retorted that the reason why she praised Ali and condemned him was that, whereas Ali was not using state funds for bringing people to his side, Moaviya was playing ducks and drakes with the funds of the treasury over which he had no right and which were held by him, according to the Prophet's ruling, in trust for the people of the Muslim State. Enraged at this, Moaviya had expelled her from Damascus after subjecting her to inhuman tortures. Undeterred by all this she had continued to praise Ali and his family. When her son Wahab was born late in her life, she had thought it her duty to inculcate in him love of Ali and his sons. She was always telling him from his childhood, day in and day out, that if an occasion arose, he should not in the least hesitate to lay down his life in defence of Ali's sons. As if by premonition, she knew that, sooner or later, there would arise a conflict between the forces of evil and oppression as represented by Moaviya and his profligate son Yazid, and forces of righteousness and Islamic virtues represented by the sons of Ali. When she was informed by Wahab that Husain, with a few faithful followers, was facing overwhelming odds, she asked her son to hurry to his aid. All three of them came over to Husain and the mother besecched Husain to let Wahab join his fight against Yazid's battalions. When

Husain learnt that Wahab had got married only a couple of days before, he insisted on him to leave him and seek safety with his wife and mother. That brave son of a brave mother would not, however, agree to this "O Imam," he said with his head bowed, "how is it possible for me to leave you and your dear ones in this condition? If I leave you and go away, my conscience would ever sting me for failing to do my duty." He was able to convince Husain that he had made up his mind and nothing could make him change his decision.

There was in Husain's camp Muslim Ibne Ausaja, a venerable companion of the Prophet. Age had bent his back but nor dampened his zeal for the cause of truth. He had seen the Prophet fondly kissing Husain. He had seen the Prophet getting down front the pulpit in the mosque at Medina in the midst of a sermon if Husain fell down by tripping over the date-leaf mat. He had beheld the Prophet's perturbation if Husain, during his childhood, cried on account of any pain suffered by him. He had been a witness to the sight when, on an Idd day, the Prophet had gone through the streets of Medina carrying Hasan and Husain on his two shoulders and uttering cries of a camel, to please these beloved children who wanted to have a camel ride. He had heard one of the Prophet's companions exclaim in amazement ar this sight: "What a wonderful mount these children have got!" and the Prophet's prompt reply: "Nay, do not say that. You may rather say what excellent riders I have get." This aged follower of Husain could not even bear the thought of leaving Husain in this hour of trial, though Husain did his best to convince him that, at his age of more than four score and ten, engaging in a battle was unthinkable. Though age had physically withered him, his enlightened spirit sustained him and added to his unswerving determination to fight for Husain and shed his blood to the last drop.

There was Buraire Hamadani, that brave warrior whose prowess in single combat had become legendary. When he saw that Amr Saad and his men had made up their mind to kill Husain and his kinsmen, he was itching to give them a taste of his sword which had always struck terror in his enemies' hearts. With difficulty Husain was able to restrain him and convince him that his purpose was not to attack the enemy but to defend and die like martyrs. This brave warrior had called a meeting of the 53 other followers of Husain on the eve of the 10th of Muharram and urged them to guard Husain and his people against any ambush or surprise attack. He had cautioned them that the enemy, who were known for their stealthy and crafty tactics, might make a surprise attack during the night and kill Husain and, if this happened during their lifetime, an indelible stigma would attach to all of them which nothing they would do, could wipe out. It was Burair who, while standing guard outside Husain's tent, had overheard the talk between Husain and his sister Zianab, when she had enquired anxiously from him whether his followers, who were with him, would fight for him or leave him. He had, on hearing this, called his other companions and, with bowed head, assured Zainab that each of them considered it a great honour to fight for her brother and die for him. In token of their earnestness, at his instance, each follower had broken the sheath of his sword by way of assurance to Zainab that they would not put back the sword in their scabbards till death came to them.

It was this brave Burair who, during his rounds of the

camp, had heard the cries of the thirsty children for water and had called a few of the friends of Husain to make arrangements to bring at least one bag full of water to wet the dry lips of the children. He and the gallant few had marched towards the river bank with determination to get water, cost what it might. When challenged by the soldiers of Amr Saad, who were guarding the river banks, and being asked as to who he was and for what he had come, he had boldly told them that he was Buraire Hamadani, follower of Husain, and had come to take water from the river to Husain's camp for the thirsty children of the Imam. "We have not the least objection to you and your friends drinking as much water as you want," they had replied, "but we cannot allow you to take a drop of water lor Husain's children." How infuriated he had got at this reply and shouted back at them: "Oh heartless brutes you have no consideration for the helpless children of Husain whom thirst is killing by inches? So long as these innocent children do not get water, it is unthinkable for any of us to taste even a drop of it." When they mockingly rejected his request, full of rage and full of grief, he had added: "If that is your final reply, be ready to fight us, for we shall not go back without water, whatever the consequences." With what bravery he and a handful of his friends had fought and dispersed the regiment that was guarding the river, and with what satisfaction he had filled the bag with water and hurried towards the camp, defending agiinst the onslaughts of the soldiers who had scurried there to prevent water being carried to the children! How with pride and satisfaction he had placed the bag of water at the feet of the thirsty children who had stampeded round the water-bag with shouts of joy and thrown themselves on it! With what dismay and dejection he had seen the tied end of the bag opening under the crush of the thirsty children and water flowing out on the dry soil, and the children crying with disappointment and rubbing their bodies on the wet sand! Moved to tears at this heart-rending sight, how he had exclaimed in utter despondency: "Alas, Burair's efforts have gone in vain and the thirst of these innocents has remained unquenched!"

Husain's depleted army, if it is permissible to give that nomenclature to that handful of warriors, had an eleventh hour addition. It was Hur, son of Yazide Riyahi, who had come over to Husain's side on the eve of the battle of Karbala. This brave warrior, who commanded a battalion in the army of Amr Saad, had his first encounter with Husain on his way to Karbala. Hur's forces had exhausted their water supply whilst proceeding to meet Husain and his men with the intention of preventing him from proceeding towards Kufa and bringing him to the plain of Karbala. His men and horses were so thirsty that their tongues were jutting out from their mouths. When Husain saw this conditions of Hur's men, he offered to them the water which he was carrying with him. Husain and Abbas personally supervised this operation and not only gave to Hur's men all the water they needed but also allowed their horses to drink to their fill. After this Hur had asked Husain to proceed towards the plain of Karabla. In spite of Husain's protestations, he had remained adamant. Husain, knowing that this brave soldier was acting according to his superior's instructions, without realising the coscqucnccs of his actions, agreed to divert his route.

When Hur cut off Husain's route and forced him to proceed to Karbala, he was under the belief that a peaceful solution could be found in the course of negotiations with Amr Saad. Little did he realise that the army of Syria would dare to spill the blood of the Prophet's grandson and his beloved ones. Only on the night of the 9th of Muharram, when an announcement was made by Amr Saad and Shimr that on the next day no quarter would be given to Husain and his men, he realised what a great mistake he had made in forcing Husain to come to Karbala against his will. He was overcome by repentance. Contrition was gnawing at his heart. He realised that Husain had nothing her peaceful intentions for, had that not been the case, he could have easily defeated him when he had intercepted Husain's men even after giving water to his men and beasts. He had himself pleaded with Amr Saad to make water available to Husain and his kinsmen and thirsty children, narrating the incident of Husain providing water to his men when they were on the verge of collapse on account of thirst, aggravated by the hear of the desert. But all his pleadings and persuasions had been in vain. Whatever he had urged, had fallen on deaf ears,

Hur was pacing the floor of his tent like a caged lion. Repentance was earing up the heart of this gallant soldier at the realisation that he was instrumental in placing in this dangerous state Husain, whom he had in his heart of hearts always admired and respected. He was shaking with rage like a twig in a field facing a gust of wind. He was now conscious of the fact that the least he could do was to go over to Husain and offer to die in defending him before any of his other friends and followers. One of his colleagues, who saw him in this agitated state while peeping into his tent, asked him with great surprise: "Well, Hur, I know that most of the soldiers and officers in our camp are trembling in their shoes at the thought of fighting against the brave sons and grandsons of Ali rommorrow. But I thought you would be an exception and would not be frightened by the thought of meeting your death on the battle-field." He replied with disdain in his voice: "I am not afraid of facing death, but I shudder to think what perdition I shall have to face on the Day of Resurrection if I fought against the grandson of the Prophet who was my benefactor when my men and I were at his mercy and were overpowered by thirst. What answer will I be able to give to my Maker on the Day of Judgment when he will ask me why I had betrayed my own benefactor?"

It did not take Hur very long to resolve his mental conflict. It was a difficult choice for him — either to choose the worldly gains, the fishes and loaves of office, power and pelf which he would get in plenty by remaining in Yazid's army, or to accept certain death which awaited him in case he went over to Husain's camp. It was a choice between hell and heaven and he unhesitatingly chose the latter without any mental reservations. He revealed his intentions to his son and faithful slave. Both of them whole-heartedly agreed with his choice and decided to cross over to Husain's side regardless of the consequences. All three of them mounted their horses and rode towards Husain's camp. Before reaching the outskirts of Husain's camp, they dismounted from their horses. They were hearing a hum of prayers from the tents of Husain's followers and frequent cries of thirsty children. Hur felt that he was responsible for bringing Husain and his family to this state and whatever he did, could not remove the stigma that would forever attach to him for the role he had played in bringing Husain to

Karbala. He asked his son to tie up his hands so that he could surrender himself to Husain and abjectly ask for his forgiveness.

Seeing all three of them approaching towards their camp, Husain and Abbas came forward. Hur fell down on his knees and begged Husain to forgive him for what he had done. "Had I known that my action on that day would come to such a pass," he said, "I would never have so obstinately insisted on your changing your route." With tears in his eyes he entreated: "O Husain, my master, I consider my crime so heinous and unpardonable that I cannot even dare to ask you for your forgiveness. The least I can do now is to lay down my life first, before any one from amongst you is killed. I have brought my son with me to die in defending your sons. I throw myself on your mercy and implore you to forgive me as, without your pardon, I can never redeem my soul."

Husain was deeply moved by Hur's words. Advancing towards him, he embraced him with a cordiality peculiar to him and said: "Hur, my noble friend, I do not in the least blame you for what you have done. The strength of character you have displayed by spurning all worldly gains and all the tempting allurements of this worldly life which would have come to you, had you remained on the other side, has added inches to your moral stature. If there is at all anything to be forgiven, I have already forgiven you. Nay, I consider you to be my honoured guest. My regret is that I cannot do anything for you all at this time when, contrary to having means of entertaining you, we do not have even a morsel of food or a drop of water to offer you."

Hur was rendered speechless at this display of generosity. He had heard so much of the forgiveness and other noble traits in the character of the grandsons of the Prophet but he was surprised that, without a word of reproach, without the least castigation, without the least bitterness or rancour, Husain had welcomed him with open arms.

Like moths hovering round a candle, Husain's companions and kinsmen surrounded him throughout the night. It was a sleepless night for them every minute of which was spent in the remembrance of the Creator or in exhorting one another to see that no harm came to Husain so long as any of them was alive. With the breaking of dawn, Ali Akbar gave the call for morning prayers. As they were making preparations for their prayers, a volley of arrows greeted them from the enemy's side. Amr Saad was the first to fling the arrow in Husain's direction, after calling his men to bear witness to his act before Yazid. Blinded by the lure of rewards, he began the day with a despicable deed which was to condemn him and his name till eternity.

Seeing the hostile actions of the enemy, Husain's friends and companions held hasty consultations and decided that a few of them should stand round Husain while the rest of the congregation engaged in prayers, so that no harm was done to them by the enemy's arrows. Standing as shields in front of the Imam, these brave soldiers were moving from side to side, not to dodge the arrows, but to receive them on their bodies so that those engaged in prayers may not be wounded. When the prayers were over, about 23 of Husain's soldiers were seriously wounded.

With the rising of the sun, the enemy started beating battle-drums. Above the din of the battle-drums rose the cries of enemy soldiers challenging Husain to send his men for combats with them. Hur was adamantly insisting that he and his son and slave, whom he loved as much as his son, should be allowed to go first. Perhaps he had at the back of his mind the idea that the battalion of 1,000, which he had commanded in Amr Sand's army, could be moved by his appeal on Husain's behalf and, if he succeeded in making them waver, the others too might follow suit. He had some ray of hope that he might be able to save the day and undo what he had done by bringing Husain to Karbala.

Mounting his horse on getting permission from Husain, Hur marched out with his son and slave. Pausing before the army of Yazid, he delivered a harangue full of eloquence and persuasion. He told the enemy soldiers that only till the previous night he was with them but when the realisation of what he was doing had dawned on him, he had decided to go over to the side of truth and justice represented by Husain. He told them that at that time he had felt as if he was poised on the top of a huge ridge of fate, on one side of which lay heaven and on the other hell; that he had made the choice realising that this world was transitory and all that it offered was ephemeral. He eloquently urged them to realise that all the bewitching things and adornments which life offered them were like apples of Sodom, good to look at, but gall and worm-wood to the taste, he quoted to them verses from the Quran o the effect that killing of an innocent camel of a Prophet of yore had brought down the wrath of God. He asked them to reflect on what their killing of the beloved grandson of the Prophet of Islam, whom he had loved and adored so much, would bring down on them. His words cast a magnetic spell on the forces which were erstwhile under his command. Shimr realised that all would be lost if Hur was allowed to speak further to the army under his command. He whispered to Amr Saad to order his men to attack Hur, his son and slave without meeting them in single combats, though such an attack was contrary to the accepted rules of battles in those days. Amr Saad at once ordered his army to launch a mass attack on the three of them and promised fabulous rewards to those who succeeded in killing them. The cupidity of those hirelings of Yazid was aroused and, forgetting everything, they fell upon Hur, his son and slave. All three of them wielded their swords in defence. Such was their skill with the sword that, though hopelessly outnumbered, they killed enemy soldiers by dozens. Tearing the enemy ranks, Hur rushed through them dexterously using his sword. Very soon the odds began to tell against all three of them. First to fall was Hur's son and then his slave. Hur had advanced a considerable distance fighting the foes on both sides of him. Exhausted with the flow of blood from a deep head wound, he became giddy and fell over from his horse. Even at that moment he had a desire to hear from Husain's lips once again that he had forgiven him. Mustering all his strength he shouted for Husain before he struck the ground and became unconscious.

On hearing Hur's cry Husain and Abbas rushed out from the camp, swords in hand. Piercing the enemy ranks, they reached the place where Hur was lying. Husain lifted his head and put it in his lap. He cleansed the blood and tied his kerchief, which had been woven by his mother Fatima with her own hands, as a bandage for the wound. Hur opened his eyes and looked straight into

Husain's eyes. Though he was speechless, his eyes conveyed to Husain his message. Husain understood and affectionately put his hand on Hur's head exclaiming: "May God bless you for the noble role you have played today in befriending me." Hearing these words Hur breathed his last with his head still resting in Husain's lap. Husain and Abbas lifted the dead body and carried it to the camp.

After Hur came the turn of the other devoted friends of Husain. Each of them was vying with the others to sacrifice his life first. Each seemed to be burning with the desire to die in defending Husain and his beloved ones, Habib Ibne Mazahir, Muslim Ibne Ausaja, Buraire Hamadani, Zohair Ibne Kain, Jawn and others went out to fight against tremendous odds, floored many warriors in single combats, and fell fighting bravely against the attack of a host of enemies. Each of them called Husain as he fell from horseback: "My master, I convey to you my last salutations." On each occasion Husain, with Abbas, Akbar, and his other followers and friends, rushed out to be on the side of his dying friend. His friends would ask their dying brethren whether they had any last wish to convey. The invariable reply was: "Yes, so long as you are alive, see that no harm comes to Husain or any member of his family." Those of them who were rendered speechless would just point towards Husain and by signs convey to the others that their last wish was that all the companions should fight to the bitter end in defence of Husain so that at least, so long as they were alive, no enemy could dare to inflict any wounds on Husain.

There was a regular procession of dead bodies coming to the morgue in Husain's camp. From early in the morning

Husain was lifting the bodies of the martyrs, his faithful defenders and carrying them to his camp assisted by Abbas, Ali Akbar and the others. He was insisting on doing this himself because he considered this to be the least he could do for those noble souls who had displayed love and devotion for him in these most trying circumstances the like of which the world had not witnessed. In this way he carried the bodies of Muslim Ibne Ausaja, Zohair Ibne Kain, Buraire Hamadani, Jawn, Habib Ibne Mazahir, and the rest. He used to weep copiously over their dead bodies, remembering their love and affection for him, their deep devotion and their spirit of sacrifice. The death of each faithful friend was proving a cripppling blow for Husain. These brave soldiers did not have their families with them in Karbala who could mourn their death; but Husain's sisters and daughters and the ladies of his house were mourning their death as if they were their own brothers and sons.

Wahab Ibne Abdullah Kalabi, the young newly-married warrior who had joined Husain's camp was the last to go. Every time he was coming to Husain and begging him for permission to go to the battle-plain and die fighting, but Husain was holding him back. When all of Husain's faithful friends were exhausted, this young lad fell at Husain's feet and entreated him to let him go. Husain told him that, since he had his mother and newly-wed wife with him, he should secure their permission because he owed a duty to them. The mother of Wahab, who was nearby, heard this and told the Imam that since that morning she had been insisting upon her son to fight in defence of Husain before all the others. "I have nourished him with my milk in his childhood," she said, "and I shall consider him my son only if he dies defending you as the others have done." According to Husain's bidding Wahab went to his bride to seek her permission. With tears in her eyes she said to him: "It is your first and foremost obligation to defend the Prophet's grandson and his family even at the cost of your life. I hope to meet you in heaven. I expect you to meet me at the threshold of heaven and to pray that our meeting there may not be long delayed." Afrer a short silence she added reflectively, "I know that the enemy will not spare a single male member of Husain's family and they will make us women captives, it is very likely that they will show some respect to the ladies of Husain's family out of regard for the Prophet; but they may not show the same consideration to me and your mother. I only want you to request the Imam that he may leave us with the ladies of his family so that we may be treated with the respect that will be accorded to them." Husain assured Wahab that his wife and mother would he looked after by Zainab and Kulsum and the other ladies of his house. Little did Wahab's wife realise that the heartless soldiers of Yazid would treat the ladies of the Prophet's house worse than ordinary captives and slaves! Wahab went out into the battle-field and died fighting gallantly like the rest of his companions.

History of mankind is replete with instances where brave persons have risen to great heights fighting for noble causes. There are instances where out of love and affection, or sense of duty and devotion, people have endured hardship and sufferings and died in defence of ideals they cherished. But never before or after deeds of such selfless devotion and self abnegation have been witnessed as in Karbala on that memorable day. How truly Hur had spoken to the army of Yazid that in this transitory world nothing endures forever and death is the inevitable goal of every living soul. The hirelings of Yazid, who for the sake of worldly gains shed the blood of innocent martyrs, are all dead and forgotten, and not a stone tells where they lie. The names of those who played a leading role in conducting the carnage on that day, are remembered with feelings of contempt and disgust. The remembrance of their dastardly deeds evokes feelings of revulsion. On the other hand what the friends and followers of Husain did in the battle of Karbala has made their names immortal. Their heroic deeds are recalled and narrated every year during the month of Muharram throughout the length and breadth of Islamic countries and communitties. Even in death they lie buried around Husain and his sons. Habib Ibne Mazahir's grave in the entrance-hall of Husain's Mausoleum conveys the impression that, even in death, this faithful friend of Husain is serving the duties of a sentinel as he did on the eve of the battle of Karbala. Each of them had lived a noble life and died a noble death.

Akbar, the Hashimite Prince

The whole town of Medina was looming with activity. People from all parts of the town were looking into the street of the Hashimites where a caravan was getting ready or a journey. The elders of the town were talking to each other in hushed tones, recalling the words of the Prophet, that a day will dawn when his beloved grandson Husain will leave Medina with his sons, brothers, nephews and kinsmen never to return. There was sadness on the faces of all, young and old. The elderly people were aghast at the thought of Husain going away forever. They were accustomed to turning to him in all their needs. The youths of Medina were saddened by the thought of Abbas and Ali Akbar and Qasim going away for good. Their anxious enquiries could only elicit this much information that Husain, with his kinsmen and children, was going for Hajj and from there to an unknown destination.

Thoughts of parting were tormenting not only the male population of Medina but also the womenfolk of the town. They too were accustomed to the munificence of the ladies of the Prophet's house. Who was there amongst them who had not received help and counsel from the daughters of Fatima? Who would be left now to whom they could turn in their hour of need, when Zainab and Kulsum, Umme Rubab and Umme Leila had left Medina? Had not times out of number their children received gifts and favours from Sakina and Rokayya?

As was their wont, the people of Medina, men and women, young and old, had gone to the tomb of the Prophet to pray and seek solace — to pray to God with the invocations of his Prophet that they may be spared the ordeal of separation from Husain and his family. There at the tomb of the Prophet they witnessed a heart-rending scene. They saw Husain and Zainab, prostrate with grief and sorrow, bidding farewell to the Prophet. They saw both of them visiting the grave of Fatima and lamenting over the separation, as if they were parting forever.

It was rumoured that Husain was leaving Medina to arrange the marriage of his son Ali Akbar with some Princess, some lady of a noble stock in some distant land. Could this rumour be correct? They all knew that there was not a young lad of marriageable age in Arabia who could be said to be fit to hold a candle before him. His handsome looks were matched by his handsome deeds. His nobility of character, his sense of duty, his generosity, his chivalry, his geniality, his love of justice and fairplay had endeared him to every soul. It was a well-known fact amongst the Arabs throughout Hedjaz that Ali Akbar was bearing a remarkable resemblance to the Holy Prophet. In looks, in voice, in mannerism, in gait and in every way, he resembled the Prophet. The resemblance was so marked that people from far and wide were coming to see him, to he reminded of the Prophet whom they were missing so much. Those who had not bad the good fortune to see the Prophet were told by their elders that Ali Akbar was the very image of Muhammad, may Peace of Allah be on him. There could, therefore, be no room for doubt that the noblest families of Arabia would consider it a signal honour if this scion of the Prophet's family were to ask for their daughter in marriage. But then, if Husain and his family were leaving Medina for Ali Akbar's marriage, they would not be secretive about it. The Prophet's grandson would in that case have given out the good tidings to the public. There was not a living being in that town whose heart would not have been filled with joy to hear about the betrothal of Ali Akbar. And if marriage of Ali Akbar was the purpose, surely Husain would not choose this season when, outside the oasis of Medina, the scorching heat of summer was baking the desert sands!

After long discussions, by a consensus of opinion, it was decided to approach Husain in a delegation and to dissuade him from undertaking the journey. Some of the venerable companions of the Prophet undertook to apprise Husain of their forebodings and their recollection of his grandfather's prophecy that, if Husain migrated from Medina with his family, he would not return.

The caravan was almost ready to depart. The horses were neighing with impatience and champing their bits in the oppressive heat of that day. Husain was standing near his horse intently watching the arrangements being made by Abbas and Ali Akbar. He was reflectively following their movements as they were helping each lady and each child to mount the camels, as they were lending a helping hand to the ladies with tender care and affection; as the ladies were graciously and profusely thanking them for the excellent arrangements they had made for their comforts and for protecting them from the unbearable heat by holding their own gowns over their heads as a canopy. This sight had some inexplicable effect on Husain, for his eyes were glittering with tears. The solicitude displayed by his brother and son for the ladies and children should have field him with happiness; bur instead, the effect on him was just the opposite. Was he beholding the shadows of some coming events?

At this moment came the representatives of the people of Medina. With one voice they entreated Husain to abandon the idea of undertaking this journey. Their leader, with supplication in his faltering voice, besought Husain to tell them why he had decided to leave them and the Prophet's tomb for which he had so much attachment. "O Son of the Prophet, if we have displeased you in any way, please forgive us." At this display of love and affection Husain was moved to tears. Suppressing his sobs he replied: "My dear brethren, believe me that my heart is bleeding at this parting — parting from you and from the graves of my beloved grandfather, my dearest mother and my brother, whom I held dearer than my life. Had it not been for the call of duty, I assure you I would have abandoned the idea of leaving Medina. It grieves me most that I cannot for once grant you your wishes when you all love me so dearly. But Almighty Allah has so willed it and in His divine dispensation ordained that I should undertake this journey. I know what hardships await me; but the Prophet has groomed me from my childhood to face them."

Seeing that the hand of destiny was snatching away Husain from them, they conferred amongst themselves and suggested that, if his decision to go from Medina was final, he should take with him all the able-bodied persons of the town so that they could protect him and his people. They reminded him of the treachery that was pervading the atmosphere in the adjoining regions. Husain, obviously moved by their sincere consideration for his safety, thanked them profusely. But he told them that, in accordance with the wishes of the Prophet, he had to fulfil the mission of his life only with those who were destined to be associated with him in the task confronting him.

When they received this reply from Husain to their

entreaties, the representatives of Medinites requested Husain to grant them one wish — to leave Ali Akbar behind him in Medina. "O Husain," they said, "we cannot bear the thought of parting with your son Ali Akbar. He is the very image of the Prophet. Whenever we feel overcome by the remembrance of Muhammad, we go to Ali Akbar to have a look at him and take comfort. We shall look after him better than we look after our own sons. We promise that we shall treat his every wish as a command. In fair weather and foul we shall stand by him. Even if we die, we shall command our children as our dying wish to attend to all his comforts and needs. His exemplary life has been an object lesson for our sons who are devoted to him as if he were their brother." These pleadings, which had a ring of sincerity and earnestness, rendered Husain quite speechless for a time. How could he tell them what was in store for Ali Akbar whom they loved and adored so much? When his sad reflections had subsided, he replied to them in a tone tinged with pathos, "Alas, I only wish I could entrust my Ali Akbar to your care! In my mission he has to play a role, the importance of which time alone will tell. I cannot accede to your request for reasons which I cannot reveal to you; but rest assured that I shall always remember your kindness to me. I shall carry with me vivid memories of this parting and remember you in my prayers."

When the heavens were glowing with the last steps of day, the caravan left on its long-drawn journey to the unknown destination. Soon darkness descended upon Medina as if symbolic of the darkness and gloom which the departure of Husain had cast on the town, associated with a myriad memories of his childhood.

****

Meandering through the desert, the caravan had reached its destitution — a destination which Allah had willed for it. The march of Husain and his kinsmen in this world had ended; but it was just the beginning of their march towards their real goal. With the dawn of the 10th day of the month of Muharram the events, for which the Prophet and Ali and Fatima had prepared Husain, started unfolding themselves. What a day it was and what fateful events it encompassed!

One by one the faithful followers went out to fight for the cause of Islam which forces of evil were attempting to stifle, and in the process faced death. In their glorious deaths they demonstrated what steadfastness and unflinching faith, what courage of conviction can achieve and attain against all odds. With his devoted supporters now sleeping the sweet slumber of death from which nothing could awaken them, the turn of Husain's sons and brothers and nephews came. In spite of Husain's best efforts to send his son Ali Akbar to the battle-field before all his devoted friends and faithful followers, they would not even let him mention it. The thought of Ali Akbar, Husain's beloved son, laying down his life in battle, when they were still alive, was too much for them. It would be blasphemous for them even to entertain such an idea!

Ali Akbar went over to his father to ask his permission to go out into that gory arena from which no person from his camp had returned. Husain looked at his face; it would be more correct to say that for a couple of minutes his stare was fixed on that face which he loved so much; which reminded him every time of his grandfather whom he resembled every inch. He tried to say something but his voice failed him. With considerable effort he whispered with downcast eyes: "Akbar, I wish you had become a father; then you would have known what I am experiencing at this moment. My son, how can a father ask his son to go, when he knows that the parting would be forever! But Akbar, the call of duty makes me helpless in this matter. Go to your mother, and to your aunt Zainab who has brought you up from childhood and loved you and cared for you more than for her own sons, and seek their permission." Ali Akbar entered the tent of his aunt Zainab. He found her and his mother Umme Laila gazing vacantly towards the battle-field and listening intently to the battle-cries of the enemy hordes. Their instinct made them aware that, now that all the devoted followers of Husain had laid down their dear lives defending him and them, the turn of his sons, and brothers and nephews had come. It was now only a question of time. It was only a question who would go first from amongst them.

The light footsteps of Ali Akbar roused both of them from their reverie. Both of them fixed their gaze on him without uttering a word. Zainab broke the silence with an exclamation: "Oh God, can it be true that Akbar has come to bid me and his mother the last farewell! Akbar, do not say that you are ready for the last journey. So long as my sons Aun and Muhammad are there, it is impossible for me to let you go."

Akbar knew what love and affection his aunt Zainab had for him. He was conscious of the pangs of sorrow she was experiencing at that moment. Her affection for him transcended everything except her love for Husain. He looked at her face, and at his mother's who was rendered speechless by her surging feelings of anguish. He knew not how to tell them that he had prepared himself for the journey to Heaven that lay ahead. He summoned to his aid his most coaxing manners that had always made his mother and Zainab accede to his requests and said: "My aunt, for all my father's kinsmen the inevitable hour has come. I implore you by the love you bear for your brother, to let me go so that it may not be said that he spared me till all his brothers and nephews were killed. Abbas, my uncle, is Commander of our army. The others are all younger than me. When death is a certainty, let me die first so that I can quench my thirst at the heavenly spring of Kausar at the hands of my grandfather." The earnestness of Akbar's tone convinced Zainab and his mother that he was determined to go. It seemed to be his last wish to lay down his life before all his kinsmen. Since on no other occasion they had denied him his wishes, it seemed so difficult to say no to his last desire. With a gasp Zainab could only say, "Akbar, my child, if the call of death has come to you, go." His mother could only say: "May God be with you, my son. With you I am losing all I had and cared for in this world. Your father has told me what destiny has in store for me. After you, for me pleasure and pain will have no difference." With these words she fell unconscious in Ali Akbar's arms.

The battle-cry from the enemy's ranks was becoming louder and louder. Ali Akbar knew that he had to go out quickly lest the enemy, seeing that their challenges for combat were remaining unanswered, got emboldened to make a concerted attack on his father's camp. Even such a thought was unbearable for him. So long as he was alive, how could he permit the onslaught of Yazid's forces on his camp where helpless women and defenceless children were lying huddled together? He gently put his mother in his aunt Zainab's arms saying: "Zainab, my aunt, I am leaving my mother to your care. I know, from your childhood, your mother Bibi Fatima has prepared you for the soul-stirring events of today and what is to come hereafter. My mother will not be able to bear the blows and calamities that are to befall her, unless you lend her your courage. I implore you by the infinite love you bear for me to show the fortitude that you are capable of, so that your patience may sustain my mother when she sees my dead body brought into the camp's morgue. I entrust her to your care because there will be none to solace her and look after her in the years of dismay and despondency that lie ahead of her." Ali Akbar embraced his loving aunt Zainab with tender love and affection for the last time. She exclaimed: "Akbar, go. My child, I entrust you to God. To ease your last moments I promise you that, so long as I live, I shall look after Umme Laila with the affection of a mother."

With a heavy heart Ali Akbar returned to his father. There was no need for him to say that he had bid farewell to his mother and aunt Zainab, for the sorrow depicted on his face spoke volumes to Husain. Silently he rose and put the Prophet's turban on Akbar's head, tied the scabbard on his waist and imprinted a kiss on his forehead. In a failing, faltering voice he muttered: "Go Akbar, God is there to help you."

Treading heavily Akbar came out of the tent with Husain following closely behind him. He was about to mount his horse when he felt somebody tugging at his robe. He could hardly see, because his eyes were almost blinded with tears. He heard the voice of his young sister Sakina supplicating him not to leave her. "O my brother," she was saying, "do not go to that battleground from which nobody has returned alive since this morning." Softly Akbar lifted her, gently and affectionately kissed her on her face and put her down. His grief was too deep for words. Husain understood the depth of Akbar's feelings and picked up Sakina to console her.

The scene of Ali Akbar's march towards the battle-field was such as would defy description. The cries of ladies and children of Husain's camp were rising above the din of battle-cries and beating of enemy drums. It was appearing as if a dead body of an only son, dead in the prime of youth, was being taken out of a house for the last rites.

****

Ali Akbar was now facing the enemy hordes. He was addressing the forces of Amr Ibne Saad with an eloquence which he had inherited from his grandfather and the Prophet. He was telling them that Husain, his father, had done them no harm and had devoted his life to the cause of Islam. He was explaining to them that by shedding the blood of Husain and his kinsmen, they would be incurring live Wrath of God and displeasure of the Prophet who had loved Husain more than any other person. He was exhorting them not to smear their hands with the blood of a person so holy, so God-fearing and so righteous. His words cast a spell on the army of the opponents. The older ones from amongst them were blinking their eyes in amazement and wondering whether the Prophet had descended from the Heavens to warn them against the shedding of Husain's blood. What a resemblance there was with the Prophet, in face, features and even mannerism! Even the voice was of

Muhammad! Bui on second thought they realised that this was Ali Akbar, the 18 year old son of Husain, about whose close resemblance with the Prophet people were talking so much.

Seeing the effect which Ali Akbar's address had produced on his soldiers, Amr Saad exhorted them to challenge him to single combat. A few of them, coveting the honour and rewards they would ger if they overpowered and killed this brave son of Husain, emaciated by three days of hunger and thirst, came forward to challenge him. One by one he met them in battle, gave them a taste of his skill and prowess in fighting and flung them from their horseback to meet the doom they so much deserved. Now it was his turn to challenge the warriors of Yazid to come forward. Seeing that in spite of his handicaps, he was capable of displaying valour and battle-craft for which his grandfather Ali had acquired name and fame and which had struck terror into the hearts of enemies of Islam, none dared to come forward.

Ali Akbar had received several gaping wounds in the course of his victorious single combats. He was fast losing blood and the effect of his thirst was getting accentuated with every second that was passing. He realised that the treacherous enemies would attack him en-masse. He had left his mother in a dazed condition. An irresistible urge to see his dear ones for the last time seized him and he turned his horse towards his camp.

He found his father standing at the doorstep of the tent and his mother and aunt standing inside the tent. Husain had been watching the battles of this thirsty youth and the two ladies were watching his face; they knew that if any calamity befell Ali Akbar, Husain's expression would indicate it. Whilst watching Husain's face, they were both praying — offering silent prayers: "O Allah, Who brought back Ismail to Hajra; O Allah, Who granted the prayers of the mother of Musa and restored her son to her; O Allah, Who reunited Yakoob with his son Yousuf in response to the aged father's supplications, grant us our one wish — to see Ali Akbar for once." Was it the effect of these prayers that brought back Ali Akbar to the camp?

Ali Akbar was now facing his aged father and his loving mother and Zainab. With an exclamation of joy and relief they clung to him. Husain lovingly embraced his son saying: "Bravo, my son. The gallantry you have displayed today reminded me of the battles of my revered father, Ali. The only difference was that, during his fighrs, my father Ali had not to battle against hunger and thirst as you had to." Ali Akbar with his head bent replied: "Father, thirst is killing me because my wounds have added to its effect. It is usual to ask for rewards from parents for celebrating victories in single combats and I would have asked for a cup of refreshing water from you. But alas! I know that you have not even a drop of water with which you can quench the thirst of the young children. Father, knowing this, I shall not embarrass you by asking for water. I have come only to see you and my dear ones for the last time."

Ali Akbar met each and everyone of his family. The second parting was sad as the first one — perhaps sadder. Without being told, everyone realised that this was the last time they were beholding Akbar. Fizza, the faithful maid of Fatima and Zainab was as disconsolate with grief as Zainab and Umme Laila. Husain followed Ali Akbar out of the tent. As he rode away, Husain walked behind him with a brisk pace for some distance, as a man follows his sacrificial lamb in Mina. When Akbar disappeared from his sight, he turned heavenwards and, with his hands raised, he prayed: "O Allah, Thou an my Witness that on this day I have sent away for sacrifice one whom I loved and cherished most, to defend the cause of righteousness and truth." He sat on the ground as if trying to listen expectantly to some call from the battle-field.

It was not very long before he received a wailing call, a call from Ali Akbar, a call of anguish and pain: "Father, Akbar has fallen with a mortal wound in his chest. Father, come to me for I have not long to live. If you cannot reach me, I convey my last salutations to you and my dear ones." Though Husain was anticipating such a call what ghastly effect it had on him! He rose from the ground and fell; he rose again and fell again. With one hand on his heart he struggled to his feet. Torrential tears were flooding his eyes. He rushed in the direction from which the cry had come. It seemed as if Husain's strength had ebbed away on hearing that fateful cry of his dearest son, for he was falling at every few steps. He was sobbing: "Akbar, give me another shout so that I can follow its direction. Akbar, my sight is gone with the shock I have received and there is nobody to guide me to where you lie." Abbas came rushing to the aid of his master. Holding his hand he led him on to the place from where Akbar's dying cry had come.

Now Husain was stumbling his way onwards resting his hands on Abbas' shoulders. The distance seemed interminable but at last Husain and Abbas reached the place where Akbar was lying in a pool of his own blood.

Ah, that tragic sight! May no father have occasion to see his young son in such a condition! With one hand on his chest covering a deep wound from which blood was gushing out, with his face writhing with pains, Akbar was lying on the ground prostrate and unconscious. With the agony he was enduring on account of the wound and the thirst that he was suffering, he was digging his feet into the sand. With a cry of anguish Husain fell on the body of Akbar. "My son, tell me where you are hurt; tell me who has wounded you in the chest. Why don't you say something? My Akbar, I have come in response to your call. Say one word to me, Akbar." Seeing that Akbar was lying there without any response to his entreaties, Husain turned to Abbas and said: "Abbas, why don't you tell Akbar to say something to me. My dutiful son, who used to get up on seeing me, is lying on the ground pressed by the hand of death." Husain once again flung himself on the body of Akbar. His breathing was now heavier, a gurgling sound was coming from his throat. It seemed that his young life was engaged in an uneven struggle with death. Husain put his head on Akbar's chest. He lifted it and put his own cheeks against Akbar's and wailed, "Akbar, for once open your eyes and smile, as you were always smilling to gladden my heart." Though Akbar did not open his eyes, a faint smile appeared on his lips as if he had listened to his father's request. With that sweet smile still playing on his lips, he heaved a gasp and with that his soul departed. The cheeks of the father were still touching the checks of the son, in death as so many times in life.

On seeing his son, his beloved son, breathe his last in his own hands, Husain's condition became such as no words can describe. For quite some time he remained there weeping as only an aged father who has lost a son, in his prime of youth, in such tragic circumstances, can weep. Abbas sat there by his side shedding tears. What words of consolation he could offer when the tragedy was of such a magnitude? All words of solace and comfort would sound hollow and be in vain when a father, an aged father, gives vent to his pent up emotions. After a time, Abbas reverentially touched Husain on his shoulders and reminded him that, since he had rushed out of the camp, Zainab and the other ladies of his house were waiting for him, tormented by anxiety, demented by the thoughts of the tragedy that had befallen them. Only mention of this was enough for Husain. He knew that, as the head of the family, it was his duty to rally by the side of the grief-stricken mother, his grief-stricken sister Zainab, and the children for whom this bereavement was the greatest calamity.

Husain slowly rose from the ground and tried to pick up the dead body of Akbnr but he himself fell on the ground. Abbas, seeing this, bent over him and said: "My master, Abbas is still alive by your side. How can I leave you to carry the body of Akbar and remain a silent spectator? Let me carry his body to the camp." "No Abbas," replied Husain, "let me do this as a last token of my love. To hold him by my heart, even in his death, gives me some comfort, the only comfort that is now left to me." Saying this, he made all the efforts that he was capable of and, assisted by Abbas, he lifted the body of Akbar. Clasping it close to his bosom, he started the long walk to his camp, How he readied his camp it is difficult to say. It would not be too much to imagine that his grandfather Muhammad, his father Ali, his brother Hasan and perhaps his mother Fatima had descended from heaven to help him in this task.

Husain reached the camp and laid down Akbar's body on the ground. He called Umme Laila and Zainab and Kulsum, Sakina and Rokayya, Fizza and the other ladies of the house to see the face of Akbar for the last time. The loving mother came, the loving aunts came, the children came, and surrounded the body of Ali Akbar. They looked at Akbar's face and then at Husain's. They knew that their weeping would add to Husain's grief which was already brimful. Ali Akbar's mother went up to her husband and, with stifled sobs and bent head, she said to him: "My master, I am proud of Akbar for dying such a noble death. He has laid down Itis life in the noblest cause and this thought will sustain me through the rest of my life. I implore you to pray for me, to pray for all of us, that Almighty Allah may grant us patience and solace." Saying this she turned to the dead body of her son lying on the ground and put her face on his. Zainab and Kulsum, Sakina and Rokayya had all flung themselves on Akbar's body. The tears that were flowing from their eyes were sufficient to wash away the clotted blood from the wounds of Akbar.

Husain sat for a few minutes near the dead body of his son; the son whom he had lost in such tragic circumstances; the son who had died craving for a drop of water to quench his thirst. He felt dazed with grief. He was awakened from his stupor by Qasim, the son of his brother, who had come to seek his permission to go to the battle-field. He rose from the ground, wiped the tears from his aged eyes and muttered "*Verily from God we come, and unto Him is our return.*"

The Youths of Karbala

'The days of our youth are ihe days of our glory'. What hopes and feelings surge in young hearts during this time of life! How every nerve and sinew quivers with the joy of living! Bur there are some youths to whom the cup of life is dealt in another measure. There are some budding flowers that are destined to be swept away by the hot desert winds before they have the opportunity to bloom. Such was the destiny of Husain's three nephews who were gathered outside the tents on the eve of that eventful day of Muharram.

Qasim, Aun and Muhammad were gathered to discuss the part they would play on the following day in defence of their uncle. There was grim determination writ large on their young faces. They were watching the progress of the moon as it was marching slowly through that cloudless sky, anxiously waiting for the morrow to unfold its events. Each one of them had the desire to go first into the battle-field to shed his blood. Even the few words they exchanged amongst themselves pertained to their anxiety lest their uncle Husain may hold them back. They were discussing among themselves how to secure the permission of the Imarn to march off into the battle-field.

Their talks were interrupted by someone coming and informing Qasim that his mother Umme Farwa wanted him to see her. He hurried to the tent. As soon as he entered it, his mother put her arms round him and said: "Qasim my son, do you know why I called you? I want to remind you about your duty towards your uncle, Husain. I want to tell you something about the unparalleled love and affection Hasan, your father had for Husain. The two of them were so much devoted to each other that they were always thinking and acting in unison. The slightest pain suffered by one was instantaneously felt by the other as if they were twins from the same embryo. With the unique love your father had for Husain, I can well imagine how he, if alive, would have felt today! He would have been the first to sacrifice his life for his beloved younger brother."

She stopped for a few seconds and then, in a soft tone, as if reminiscing, added: "I am sure he wanted you to deputise for him on this day. My child, when he passed away, you were too young to understand life. On his death-bed his last words to me were: 'Umme Farwa, I entrust you and my children to God and Husain. When Qasim grows up, you tell him that my dying desire was that he should stand by Husain through thick and thin. I can see the clouds of treachery gathering against Husain. A day may come when he may need the unflinching devotion and sacrifice of his near and dear ones. Though I will not live to see that day, as my last wish I want you to prepare Qasim for it from his childhood'." Her voice choked with emotion, as she continued: "My Qasim, since the day your father breathed his last, Husain has looked after you as his own son. Nay, he has treated you on all occasions better than his own sons. You know how he has fulfilled your every wish so that you may not miss the love and affection of your father. Now it is your turn to show that you can repay, to some extent, your debt of gratitude by laying down your life for him before any of his sons, brothers and kinsmen. Now is your chance to reciprocate his love and affection, by demonstrating to the enemies that you are a scion of the House of Ali and can wield the sword in defence of truth."

Qasim listened to his mother with his head bowed in respect. He felt very much relieved by what his mother had said to him because, he had felt very apprehensive as to how his mother would react when he approached her for her permission to go for the fight. He knew how his morher was attached to him after his father's death. He was well aware how restless she used to become, if she would not see him even for a few hours. He had thought that the very idea of her son marching out into the battle-field would make her demented. He felt as if his mother had taken a load off his head. He affectionately hugged her and said: "My dearest mother, I know not how I can thank you for what you have said to me just now. My filial affection for my uncle Husain is known to you. From my childhood I have not known what a father's love means but I know this for certain that even my father, if alive, would not have been so kind, so considerate, so affectionate to me as my uncle Husain has been to me. He has not allowed me to feel even for a moment that I am an orphan. Thanks to him, in the house my every wish has been a command. How is it possible for me, the son of Hasan, to be oblivious of my obligations to him? For me death would be far better than life without him and my dear uncle Abbas, and my cousins Ali Akbar, Muhammad and others."

Umme Farwa fell elated at the brave reply of her brave son. A painful thought passed her mind — the thought that this dear child who was so devoted to her and in whom she had reposed all her hopes, would perish on the fields of Karbala. With great efforts she controlled herself.

****

On the departure of Qasim, Aun and Muhammad

waited for some time for him to return. Then both of them returned to their tent to console their mother, Zainab, whose grief and sorrow defied description. As they entered the tent they saw her sitting on the ground with a caudle in her hand looking intently at Ali Akbar, their cousin, whom she had brought up as her own son and for whom her love and affection was without a parallel. When she saw both of them entering the tent, she beckoned to them to come and sit near Ali Akbar. Both of them did so according to her bidding. She turned towards them and said in a low tone: "My children, do you know what tomorrow has in store for us? It will be a day of trial; it will be a day when the blood of our family will flow like water; it will be a day on which all the vendetta nurtured by the enemies of the Prophet's house for all these years will be spilled out. I want both of you, my beloved sons, to defend your uncle Husain and his children at the cost of your lives." After a pause she added: "When I was leaving Mecca, your father Abdullah asked me to take both of you with me so that, if an occasion arose you Aun, could be the deputy of your father in seeking martyrdom, and you Muhammad, could be my offering in the cause of Islam."

Hearing their mother talk in this vein touched both of them to the quick. How could they tell their mother Zainab that they were fully prepared for the doom that awaited them; that they were both coveting martyrdom in defence of the cause of Islam and its inviolable principles for which Husain stood up so boldly and firmly in the face of odds! Aun was the first to speak, his voice was quivering with emotion when he said: "Mother, we both feel so elated to know that we have your permission to fight in defence of our uncle and his family. God willing, we both will show the army of Amr Saad that we are the grandsons of Jaafar-e-Tayyar whose prowess in battle had become legendary. We shall offer such fight tomorrow that, whenever you will remember us and mourn for us, your grief will be mingled with pride that we lived up to the reputation of our family."

Hardly had Aun concluded when Muhammad, the younger one, burst out saying, "My loving mother, do not think that we need any exhortation to fight valiantly tomorrow. I am itching to go out in defence of my uncle. From my childhood I have been hearing about the valour of my maternal grandfather Ali, and paternal grandfather Jaafar-e-Tayyar. It is not for nothing that we both of us have learnt the art of single combat from our uncle Abbas. You may rest assured that, so long as we breathe, we shall not let the least harm come to our uncle Husain or to any of his children."

With this reply of the brave youngsters Zainab felt reassured. It was not that she, for a moment, doubted their devotion or sense of duty. It was not that she considered it necessary to instill any courage in them, for she knew that both of them were brave and noble sons of a brave and noble father. Her love for her brave sons was surging within her. She was feeling as if her heart was getting squeezed when she was conjuring up the vision of these youths dying as martyrs.

Ali Akbar who was listening quietly to the talk between the mother and the two sons, looked at the faces of the mother and then at the sons. With a faint smile playing on his lips no said: "We of the Prophet's family will go out to meet death as is our wont. In what order it will be, it is for God to determine." When he said this, perhaps he had the conviction that Husain would never allow his nephews to die so long as he, Ali Akbar was there. How rightly he had surmised, the events of Ashura would show!

****

Like all passing things, that night also passed away to become a chapter of history. The day dawned and with it began the gory events which make mankind, who have the vestiges of humanity, tremble with rage and grief. As Ali Akbar had surmised that night, when the turn of members of the family came, Husain came over to him and, with his hand on his heart, said to him: "My son, go forward to fulfil your appointed task." Much as Zainab and Umme Farwa protested that, so long as their sons lived, they could not think of Ali Akbar laying down his life, much as Abbas pleaded to let him be the first among the Hashimites to die fighting, Husain insisted that he would send Ali Akbar as his own representative to be the first among his kinsmen. Ali Akbar went to the battle-field never to return from it.

Zainab was disconsolate on Ali Akbar's death. Now Aun and Muhammad were hovering round Husain with entreaties to let them go. Qasim was no less vehement in his supplication for the Imam's permission to die on the battle-field. To Qasim's repeated requests his uncle's reply was: "My dear child, how can I permit you to go when I know for certain that death awaits those who venture out. Your father, my beloved Hasan, had entrusted you to my care on his death-bed. My heart trembles at the very thought of sending you into the jaws of death."

This reply of Husain broke Qasim's heart. He thought that his uncle would not under any circumstances allow him to share the fate of the other martyrs. With tears in his eyes he stood there, not knowing what to do to secure Husain's permission.

At that moment Zainab came over to her brother. With folded hands she said to Husain, "My dearest brother, in my whole life I have never asked you for a favour. Now, for the first time, I am requesting you to grant me one wish; let my sons follow in the footsteps of Ali Akbar."

Husain looked at Zainab and then at her sons. With his head bent, he replied; "Zainab, my dearest sister, I find it impossible to deny your first and last request, though my granting ii makes my heart sink within me." Turning to Aun and Muhammad he said; "My dear children, go forward and fulfil your heart's desire to die like heroes. I shall soon be joining you on your journey to eternity."

At this reply the two young heroes felt delighted in the midst of unbounded sorrows. They fell at their mother's feet and asked her for her blessings. Zainab's grief at the parting with these beloved children found its way through her tears which were now pouring from her eves in torrents. She felt an urge to clasp her young sons to her bosom before they marched our on their last journey; but for fear that such display of emotion might unnerve them, she held back. She could not say anything to them in farewell. With suppressed sobs she whispered to them: "My beloved ones, may God be with you and may He grant you quick relief from the agonies that you are to endure. It is Zainab's lot to endure ignominies with no brothers, no nephews, no sons to console her. My last request to you is to fight bravely and to die bravely so that, in the midst of my unbearable sufferings in captivity, I may at least have one remembrance to console me — your bravery in the face of overwhelming odds."

She mutely watched her sons mounting their horses assisted by Husain. Her lips were moving in silent prayers; her eyes were following the horses as they galloped out into the arena. When they both got out of sight, with a sigh she sat on the sand near her tent as if lost in a reverie.

****

When Qasim saw that Aun and Muhammad had been granted permission to march out on the entreaties of their mother, he rushed to his mother's tent. Almost sobbing with disappointment, he told Umme Farwa that Aun and Muhammad had secured the Imam's permission on the intercession of their mother but he had nobody to plead on his behalf with his uncle. In utter despondency he said; "If I am not destined to be a martyr on this day, life has no charm left for me. Am I destined to be a captive and led through the streets to a prison cell?"

Seeing Qasim so bitter and dejected Umme Farwa burst into tears of grief. Controlling herself she began to think what to do to get Husain's permission for him. Her first reaction was to go over to the Imam and to implore him as his brother's widow and seek permission for Qasim. However, in a flash she remembered her husband's words to her shortly before his death. He had told her that for Qasim a time may come when he would find himself in the trough of despair and despondency and feel dejected and depressed beyond description. He had told her that, when this happened, she should deliver to him an envelope wherein he had kept a letter specially for this occasion. This she had carefully preserved and kept with her as her most cherished thing in a box. Fortunately for her, she had brought the box with her. She hastened to fetch the letter and handing over the envelope to Qasim she said: "Qasim your present plight brought back to me your father's words that a day like this would come for you and when this happened, I should deliver the letter to you." With rekindled hope and expectation Qasim took the letter from his mother's hand and opened it. In it he found two letters — one addressed to Qasim and the other addressed to Husain.

He anxiously opened the letter meant for him and read it aloud for his mother's benefit. Hasan had written in it: "My child, when this letter reaches you, I will be no more. When you read it, you will find yourself torn with a conflict between your desire to do your duty and fulfil your obligations and demonstrate your love and esteem for your uncle, and his love and affection for you compelling him to hold you back. My Qasim, I have provided for this event by arming you with a letter for my dearest brother Husain. You may deliver the letter to Husain so that he may grant you your heart's desire. There is much that I could say for this occasion but when you will read this, you will find that time separating us is not long. So hurry along, my child, as I am waiting for you with open arms to welcome you."

When he had completed reading the letter, Qasim felt choked with emotion. His mother also stood speechless with feelings surging in her heart. Both were thinking in unison how loving and thoughtful it was of Hasan to provide a solution for their dilemma. Qasim reverentially bent on the letter and kissed it. The tears rolling from his eyes fell on the writing but, instead of smearing the lettering, they lent glitter to them.

Umme Farwa was the first to get out of the reverie. She broke the silence and said: "My dearest Qasim, now that your father has come to your rescue even in death, take his letter to your uncle Husain. I have no doubt that now he will not be able to refuse you his permission for laying down your life."

Qasim could now hardly contain himself. He rushed towards the tent of Imam Husain with the letter in his hands. He found Husain standing outside Zainab's tent looking intently towards the battle-field. Abbas was by his side and Zainab was standing near the door holding up the curtain and looking at the faces of Husain and Abbas. Qasim knew that they were all watching the combats of Ann and Muhammad. How could he disturb his uncle at such a time? He stood quietly by the side of Husain and Abbas and gazed in the direction of the army pitted against his two young cousins. He could see from clouds of dust rising in the far distance that one of them had gone ahead of the other. Not so far away he could see the younger one, Muhammad, battling against a number of enemy soliders clustered round him.

Hardly a few minutes had passed in watching the battle, when they saw Aun falling from his horse and giving a cry to his uncle to come to him and carry his body. Husain, who had already borne the afflictions of his companions' death and the loss of his dearest son, Ali Akbar, seemed to wince as if he had received a stab in his chest. He turned to Zainab to see her reaction on hearing her son's last cry. Abbas and Qasim rushed to her side to hold her. As if this blow was not enough, Muhammad also fell from his horse mortally wounded and similarly shouted to Husain to come to him. Abbas and Qasim knew that for Husain to reach his dying nephews, one after the other, was too trying even for a person of his mettle who had right through the morning performed this task himself. Abbas wanted to accompany Husain and assist him in bringing the dead brothers to the camp, leaving Qasim to attend to Zainab who had collapsed with grief and sorrow on hearing the parting cry of Muahmmad. But Husain beckoned to him to remain with Zainab. Qasim tried to follow him but Husain asked him also to remain near Zainab and console her.

Husain first reached the piace where Muhammad was lying mortally wounded. He bent over his body to find that, on account of loss of blood, his young life was ebbing fast. The child was gasping heavily. His throat was so parched that even with great efforts he was not able to speak clearly. Husain put his ear near Muhammad's mouth. In a faint, faltering voice the young lad said: "My last salutations to you uncle. Tell my mother that I have lived upto her expectations and am dying bravely as she and my father wanted me. Give my last salaams to her and console her as much as you can." The efforts made by the child in saying these words appeared to exhaust him. He added after a few seconds: "I heard the cry of Aun before I fell. Now that I am beyond any help, uncle, please go over to him and see if you can do something for him before it is too late." Hardly he had said these words, his life became extinct. Husain was beside himself with grief. But he could not remain there long as he had to go over to Aun. He rushed in the direction where Aun had fallen. On reaching his body he found that he had breathed his last. He picked up his lifeless body and pressed it to his heart.

With a heavy tread, with tears flawing in torrents, the aged uncle began his march towards the camp with the body of his nephew in his arms. Abbas came rushing from the camp towards him and said, "Let me carry Aun's body to the morgue and you take Muhammad's body. My master, Abbas is still alive to share your burden and grief." Quietly he handed over Aun's corpse to Abbas and went over to pick up Muhammad's body. The two brothers, one old and one young, were each carrying the body of a young nephew. The sight was such as to evoke sorrow and grief in the hearts of the most hard-hearted persons.

On reaching their camp Husain and Abbas laid the bodies of Aun and Muhammad on the ground. Zainab who was waiting for them came over and fell on the two bodies of her sons. "My sons, my sons," she cried, "What mother is there to send her beloved ones to meet death as I have sent mine." Her face was bathed in tears. With sobs she was saying: "My darlings, you have gone from this world with your thirst unquenched. Your grandfather Ali wll be there to quench your thirst in heaven. My beloved sons, for Zainab there is still a long, weary, unending future to face without you two to lighten the burden with your brave talk." Overpowered by her grief and emotions she fell unconscious on the dead bodies.

Husain, Abbas, Qasim and the ladies who were all standing and crying by her side, gently picked up Zainab and took her to her tent. They all knew that in such a great tragedy as had befallen her, all words of consolation would only be in vain.

****

As was the practice of Yazid's army, they started beating the drums on the slaughter of the two young nephews of Husain, to herald their victory. When the beating of drums stepped, they raised the usual cry challenging the young defenders of Husain to come out into the field to face death. Now Qasim came over to Husain, who was standing near Zainab's prostrate form with his head bent. Qasim could not muster sufficient strength to say what he had come to convey to the Imam. He quietly handed over the letter of his father for Husain which he had found in the envelope given to him by his mother. Husain glanced at the handwriting on the letter and at once recognised it as his late lamented brother's. With surprise he opened the letter and eagerly read it. As he read it on, he could not control himself and burst into a cry of grief. In the letter it was written: "My beloved Husain, when this letter will be read by you, you will be surrounded by sorrows on all sides, with dead bodies of your near and dear ones strewn round you. I will not be there to lay down my life for you, Husain, but I am leaving behind my Qasim to be my deputy on this day. Husain, I beseech you not to reject my offering. In the name of love that you bear for me, I implore you to let Qasim go forth and die in your defence. Dearest brother, in spirit I am with you, watching your heroic sacrifices and sharing your woes and affliction."

Hasan's letter brought back to Husain the memories of his dear borther to whom he was devoted and he wept copiously recollecting his love and affection. What unique love Hasan had for him that, though dead, he had left this deputy in Qssim for this day!

With effort Husain controlled himself and turned to Qasim saying: "Dear child, your father's wishes, which I regard as commands for me, leave me no other alternative. March on, Qasim, as your father wished you to do. If it is so ordained that I may bear the wound of your martyrdom, I shall bow to the Will of God."

Qasim bowed reverentially and hurried to his mother Umme Farwa, who was sitting dazed with grief on receiving the sad news of Aun and Muhammad's martyrdom. As Qasim entered her tent, she raised her head and looked at him expectantly. She could see from the look of satisfaction on his grief-stricken face that he had received Husain's permission for which he had been begging so long. An exchange of looks between the mother and son confirmed to Umme Farwa that she was right. Slowly she rose and said to Qasim: "My beloved son, all these years I have been waiting for the day when you would become a bridegroom, and dressed as a groom, come to receive my blessings. It seems that fate has decreed otherwise. Qasim, I have preserved the dress your father wore on the day of his marriage with me. I had hoped that, on your wedding day, I would ask you to wear it. Now that you are going to the land of no return, my wish is that you put on that dress so that my desire to see you dressed as a groom my be fulfilled." After a pause she continued in a reflective tone: "It is the custom for grooms to apply henna on their hands. Though I have none with me, I know that you will not need it. Your hands will be dyed with your own blood." With these words she kissed her son's cheeks and embraced him. It was a long embrace, the embrace of a mother who knew that she was seeing her young darling for the last time in this world. Holding him tightly in her arms she was looking longingly at his face, as if she wanted to let his image sink into her mind's eye for ever. All partings are sad but where the parting is forever, and in such circumstances, what words can describe it?

The mother and son tore themselves from each other lest their surging love and attachment might make their parting impossible. Umme Farwa brought out the wedding garments of Hasan for Qasim to wear. Dressed in these clothes Qasim was looking the very image of Hasan. The son, followed by the mother, went over to Zainab's tent to bid her goodbye. Zainab had not completely recovered from her swoon; in her dazed mind she thought for a montent that Hasan was coming to her. So much did Qasim resemble his father in that dress that Zainab almost thought that Hasan had descended from heaven to defend his brother. It was just a flitting thought which passed away like lightning. She realised that it was Qasim who had come to her to pay his last respects. She looked at him and then at his mother who was following him. She realised with what efforts Umme Farwa was controlling her feelings. Much as her own heart was bursting with grief at this parting with her beloved brother's son, she knew that it was essential for her to control herself for the sake of Umme Farwa. With one hand on her head and the other on her heart, she came forward to bid adieu to Qasim. With hot tears rolling down her checks she kissed Qasim on his forehead saving: "Qasim, my dear child, your aged aunt had hoped that you, my dear ones, would carry my funeral bier. But it is written in Zainab's luck that she should see the young lives of her dearest ones extinguished before her. It has fallen to my lot to see you all dead before me and to carry your memories for the rest of my dreary, unending days. March on my child with the name of God."

Qasim came to Husain and reverentially kissed his hands. Seeing Qasim so keenly resembling Hasan, his dear, departed brother Husain wept bitterly. He kissed Qasim on his checks and held the horse for him to mount. Abbas came forward to do this service but Husain would not let him do so. "This is the last occasion for me to give a send-off to my Qasim and let me do this for him." He turned to Qasim and said: "Qasim, I shall not be long in joining you."

Reaching the battle arena, Qasim addressed the enemy with an eloquence which reminded many of the sermons of his grandfather Ali. With gaping mouths they were transfixed to the ground at his words of admonition on the betrayal of the Imam. Amr Ibne Saad ordered his men to challenge him to single combat, fearing that this youth's eloquence may rouse the vestiges of goodness in some of his men. Qasim fought battles with several of them and threw them from their horses as if he were a seasoned warrior and not a youth of 14, with three day's thirst and hunger. Such was his skill with the sword and horsemanship that Husain, who was watching his nephew's fighr from a hillock near his camp, burst into spontaneous acclamation. Now no warrior from the enemy ranks was coining forward to meet the challenge of this brave son of Hasan. He was now repeatedly challanging the soldiers of Amr Saad to come forward and match their skill and swordsmanship against him in single combat. Amr Saad, seeing that none of his warriors was prepared for this, ordered his soldiers to attack Qasim together. It was now a fight between one and thousands, if such a thing can at all he called a fight. How long could Qasim ward off the attacks of swords, spears, daggers and arrows coming at him from all directions? He was wounded from head to foot. When he saw that he could no longer remain in the saddle, he gave a cry offering his last salutations to his uncle Husain.

Husain, who was watching from a distance the dastardly attack of the multitude of soldiers on his helpless Qasim, heard this cry lull of agony and pain. He felt as if he had himself received all the wounds inflicted on Qasim. He unsheathed his sword and, like an enraged lion, he rushed towards the battle-field. With sword in one hand he galloped his horse cutting through the enemy hordes. Such was the fury of his charge that the enemy were reminded of the charges of Ali, his father, in the battle of Siffin, when the dexterous Lion God had singly scattered the enemy, running through them like a knife through butter, and killing hundreds with the dexterous sweeps of his sword. For safety, the remainder of the arrant cowards ran helter-skelter to save their contemptible lives. The stampede of Yazd's soldiers was such that the body of Qasim was trampled under the feet of hundreds of minions who were a disgrace to their calling. When the battle-field was cleared of the cowards and Husain reached the body of Qasim, he found that it was torn to pieces. What feelings this gruesome sight evened in Husain's heart can better be imagined than described. Husain stumbled down from his horse and fell to the ground exclaiming: "My God, what have these cowards done to my Qasim." For some time he wept with such agony that his body convulsed. After a while he took off his robe and started picking up pieces of Qasim's body. One by one he put them all in his robe and, lifting the bundle, put it on his aged shoulders and mounted the horse. As he did so, he muttered: "My Qasim, your mother had sent you out dressed as a groom. Now you are returning to your mother with your body cut to pieces." As he was marching back towards his camp, Husain was disconsolately exclaiming: "My God, has there been an instance where an uncle had to carry his own nephew's body in such a state!"

One reaching the camp Husain put down the body on the ground, He called Abbas and asked him to bring Umme

Farwa and his sisters Zainab and Kulsum to the morgue. He beseeched Fizza, his mother's devoted maid, to console Umme Farwa and Zainab, for he knew that the condition of Qasim's body might give them such a shock as would kill them.

Qasim's mother came with Zainab on one side and Umme Kulsum on the other. Fizza went over to the ladies and said: "I beseech you, in the name of my lady Fatima, to muster all the strength and courage you can to see Qasim's remains. His mortal remains may be torn and cut to pieces but remember his soul is now with my lady and Hasan, who must have welcomed him with open arms." Saying this, she opened the robe and unfolded the body. Zainab held her aching heart, Kulsum held her reeling head and Umme Farwa fell with a shriek and fainted.

What pen can narrate the grief of a mother who has lost her only son? What words can describe the agony of a mother's loving heart on seeing her son in such a state? The land of Karbala was echoing the cries of the ladies and the wailing of the children on Qasim's death. Can any one attempt to depict what was Husain's plight at that time? Resting his head on Abbas's shoulders, Husain was saying: "My God, my God if my enemies wanted to kill me, they could do so; but what my dear ones have done that they slay them so mercilessly?"

Husain stood there, for some time as if in a trance. He was brought back to the reality of the situation by Abbas who softly said to him: "My master now let me go, as others have done. I am now the commander of soliders who are no more." Husain for a moment did not reply. Then he softly muttered: "*Verily we come from God and unto Him we shall return.*"

Abbas — The Standard-Bearer of Husain

The shifting sand-dunes of Karbala were smeared with blood. Near one of such dunes, on the bank of Alkoma, lay the prostrate figure of a youth with blood gushing out from innumerable wounds. The crimson life-tide was ebbing fast. Even so, it seemed as if he was anxiously expecting somebody to come to him, to be near him before he breathed his last. Through his parched throat he was feebly calling somebody. Yes, Abbas was anxiously expecting his master to come to him before he parted with his life, as he had come to the side of all his devoted friends who had laid down their clear lives for him and in espousing his cause.

It is said that before a man's death all the past events of his life pass before his mind's eye in a flash-back. In his last moments Abbas was seeing the events of his past life. He was seeing himself as a child in Medina following Husain with a devotion which was considered unique even for a brother. He was seeing the events of that hot and sultry day in Kufa when his illustrious father Ali was addressing a congregation in the mosque and he, as a child, with his cluracteristic devotion, was looking at the face of his beloved brother watching him intently so that he could attend to his wishes as if an instant command. Seeing from the parched lips of Husain that he was feeling extremely thirsty, how he had darted out from the mosque and returned with a tumbler full of cool, refreshing water and in the hurry to carry the water as quickly as possible to quench the consuming thirst of his dearest brother, how he had spilled water on his own clothes. He was recalling how this incident had made his illustrious father stop in the midst of his speech, with tears rolling down his cheeks at the sight of his young son all wet with water. He was remembering his father's reply to the queries from his faithful followers as to what had brought tears in his eyes, that Abbas who had wetted his body with water in the process of quenching Husain's thirst would, in the not too distant future, wet his body with his own blood in attempting to quench the thirst of his young children. He was vividly seeing the scene on the 21st Ramazan, way back in 40 Hijra, when his father, mortally wounded, was lying on his death-bed and entrusting his children and dependents to the care of his eldest brother, Hasan — all except him. Seeing that his father had commended all but him to the care of Hasan — how he, a child of 12 had burst out into uncontrollable tears. His father, on hearing him sobbing, had called him to his side and given his hand in Husain's hand with the words: "Husain, this child I am entrusting to you. He will represent me on the day of your supreme sacrifice and lay down his life in defending you and your dear ones, much as I would have done if alive on that day." How his father had turned to him and affectionately told him: "Abbas, my child, I know your unbounded love for Husain. Though you are too young to be told about it, when that day dawns, consider no sacrifice too great for Husain and his children." He saw before his mind's eye that parting with his aged mother Fatima in Medina. How she had affectionately embraced him and reminded him of the dying desire of his father to lay down his life in the defence of Husain and his dear ones.

A faint smile of satisfaction flickered for a brief moment on his parched lips — a smile of satisfaction that he had fulfilled his father's wish; that he had performed his duty for which he was brought up. It just flitted for a moment and vanished as other scenes came before his mind's eye. He was re-living the events of the night before. He was seeing Shimr stealthily coming to him and talking to him about his ties of relationship; about the protection he had been promised for Abbas by rhe Commander of Yazid's forces, only if he would leave Husain and go over to Yazid's camp; about the promises of riches and rewards that he would get; how he had spurned the suggestion of Shimr with the utmost disdain to the chargin of that servile minion who had sold his soul for a mess of pottage. How he had scared away that coward by his scathing rage saying: "You worshipper of Mammon, do not think that Abbas will be lured by your tempting offer of power and pelf? If I die in defending my master, Husain, I shall consider myself the luckiest person. Oh coward, remember that valiants die but once. Nobody is born to live eternally. By betraying my master, you have betrayed the Prophet, whose religion you profess to follow. On the Day of Judgment you will be doomed to eternal perdition. I am ashamed to own any relationship with you. Had it not been for the fact that you have come here unarmed, I would have given you the chastisement you deserve for your impudence in asking me to become a turncoat." How that wretch had scampered from there seeing him roaring like an enraged lion! The drought of that unpleasant interlude contracted his brows. Or was it the excruciating pain he was suffering on account of the deep gashes he had all over his body?

Yet another scene passed before Abbas's eyes — Sakina leading 42 children, each with a dry water-bag. The children were shouting as if in chrous —"thirst, consuming thirst, is killing us." Sakina coming to him and putting her dry water-bag at his feet and saying to him:

"O uncle, I know you will do something to get water for us. Even if you can bring one bag full of water, we can wet our parched throats." He could see that thirst, aggravated by the scorching heat of the desert, was squeezing their young lives out of them. The sight of these young kids had moved him more than any other soul-stirring events of that fateful day. How he had picked up the water-bag with assurances to Sakina that he would go and bring water — God Willing, llow he had taken Husain's permission and marched out of the camp with a sword in one hand, the flag in the other, and the bag on his shoulder, with the children following him in a group upto the outer-perimeter of the camp! How Husain had repeatedly requested him to avoid fighting as much as possible and confine himself to the task of bringing water!

His thoughts switched over to the events that had preceded his fall from the horse. With the thought of procuring water for his dear little Sakina, he had charged on the enemy who held the river banks. He had run through the enemy ranks like a knife through butter. Against his surging onslaught the enemy could not stand and had run helter-skelter shouting for protection. For a moment it seemed as if Ali, the Lion of God, had descended from heaven. In no time Abbas was near the rivulet. He had jumped down from the horse and bent to fill the water-bag. When it was filled to the brim, he had taken some water in his cupped hand to drink and satisfy his killing thirst. But, on second thoughts, he had thrown the water away. How could he drink water when Sakina and the children were still withering without water? How could he be so callous as to forget that his master, Husain had not had a drop of water since the last 3 days! He had turned to his horse which had been let loose so that it could satiate its thirst. The animal had been intently looking at its master as if to say: "I too am aware that, so long as our master and his children remain without water, our thirst cannot be quenched."

With the water-bag filled he had jumped on the horseback with one thought uppermost in his mind — to get the water for the anxiously waiting children as quickly as possible. Seeing him galloping towards the camp of Husain, the enemy had turned. Somebody had shouted from the enemy ranks that if Husain and his people get water, it would be difficult to fight them on the battle-field. Though it was an uneven fight, he fought them with valour which was so characteristic of his father's. Though he was thirsty and hungry, he charged on than and scattered them. The mercenaries of Yazid were running like lambs in a fold when charged by a lion. Seeing that a frontal assault on a man so brave was not possible, they had resorted to a barrage of arrows. When arrows were coming from all sides, Abbas had only one thought in his mind — how to protect the water-bag? To him it seemed more important to protect the water-bag than his life. Seeing that Abbas was preoccupied with this thought, one treacherous foe, hiding behind a sand-dune, had rushed out and dealt a blow on his right hand and cut it off. In a flash Abbas had transferred his sword to his left hand and the standard he was bearing he had hugged to his chest. Now that the lion of Ali was crippled, the foes had found courage to surround him. A blow from an enemy's sword severed his left arm. The odds were now mounting against him. He held the bag with his teeth and protected the bag with his bent chest on the horseback. Now the paramount thought in his mind was to reach the camp somehow or the other. A silent prayer had escaped his lips: "Merciful Allah, spare me long enough to fulfil my mission." But that was not to be. An arrow had pierced the water-bag and water had started gushing out of it. Was it water that was flowing out of that bag or the hopes of Abbas? All his efforts had been in vain. After all Sakina's thirst would remain unsatisfied and all her hopes would be frustrated. The enemies who had made bold to surround him, now seeing his helpless condition, were now gathering thick round him. One of them came near him and struck a mortal blow with an iron mace. He reeled over and fell from the horse where he was lying.

He tossed on the burning sand with excruciating pain. He fell that life was fast ebbing out but his wish to see his master had remained unfulfilled. With one last effort, with all the strength that was left in him, he shouted: "O my master, do come to me before I die." As if in answer to his prayers he felt some footsteps near him. Yes, his instinct told him that it was his lord. His one eye had been blinded by an arrow and the other filled with blood and so he could not see. But he felt his master kneeling down beside him, lifting his head and taking it into his lap. Not a word was said for a few seconds because both were chocked with emotion. At last he heard Husain's voice, a half-sob, half-muffled cry: "Abbas, my brother, what have they done to you:" If Abbas could see, would he have recognised his master? With back bent and beard turned white and hoary, on hearing the parting cry of his beloved brother, Husain's plight was such that nobody could have recognised him — such was his transformation. Abbas was now feeling the loving touch of his master's hand. With effort he muttered: "You have come at last, my Master. I thought I was not destined to have a last look at you but, thank God, you are here." With these words he put his head on the sand. Tenderly Husain lifted his head and again pui it on his lap, enquiring why he had removed it from there. "My Master," replied Abbas, "the thought that when you will be breathing your last, nobody will be there to put your head in the lap and to comfort you, makes me feel that it would be better if my head lies on the sand when I die, just as yours would be. Besides, I am your slave and you are my master. It is too much for me to put my head on your lap." Husain burst into uncontrollable tears. The sight of his brother, whose name was to become a byword for devotion and unflinching faithfulness, laying down his dear life in his arms, was heart-rending.

Abbas was heard to whisper softly: "My master, I have some last wishes to express. When I was born, I had first look at your face and it is my last desire that when I die, my gaze may be on your face. My one eye is pierced by an arrow and the other is filled wilh blood. If you will clear the eye, blood from my one I'll be able to see you and fulfil my last dying desire. My second wish is that when I die you may not carry my body to the camp. I had promised to bring water to Sakina and, since I have failed in my attempt to bring her water, I cannot face her even in death. Besides, I know that the blows that you have received since morning have all but crushed you and, carrying my body to the camp, will be a heart-breaking work for you And my third wish is that Sakina may not be brought here to see my plight. I know with what love and affection she was devoted to me. The sight of my dead body lying here will kill her."

Husain sobbingly promised him that he would carry out his last wishes and added: "Abbas, I too have a wish to be fulfilled. Since childhood you have always called me master. For once at least call me brother with your dying breath." The blood was cleared from the eye, one brother looked at the other with a longing lingering look. Abbas was heard to whisper: "My brother, my brother" and with these words he surrendered his sould to his Maker; Husain fell unconscious on the dead body of Abbas with a cry: "O Abbas, who is left to protect me and Sakina after you."

The flow of Furat became dark as winter and a murmur arose from the flowing water as if to protest against the killing of a thirsty water-bearer on its banks.

From Cradle to the Grave

The mother was looking intently into the face of her child lying in the cradle. It was a face which had become ashen-pale on account of starvation. The child, although about 10 months old, was so emaciated that any person beholding it would think that it was hardly 6 months old. The child's eyes appeared to be searching for something. As if to indicate what it wanted, the child was opening its mouth and taking out its parched tongue and turning it on its lips. The mother was sitting and watching, helplessly waiting for death to come to the child and relieve it of the agony. But what mother can bear to see her child die of starvation and, what is worse, thirst unquenched? Could she not do something to get a few drops of water which could well become the life saving elixir for the child? But where could she get these few drops of precious water which her lord, Imam Husain, and his near and dear ones were denied by the army of Yazid for 3 days? Her heart was revolting against the idea of letting her young son die of thirst. For one day she had nursed the child at her breast but, as she herself had gone without the essential nourishments for so long, her milk had dried up completely and there was not a drop that she could give to the child. Not far away, the rivulet was gushing by and murmur of its rippling waters could be heard in the stillness that pervaded those afternoon hours.

A passing thought came into the mother's mind to take up the child in her arms and go out — to run to the river and snatch some water to quench the child's thirst. But it was just a flitting thought which she rejected on considering what her husband, Imam Husain, would say and feel. Would not such action on her part in going out with the child, cause great agony to her lord? Had he not suffered enough during the day — losing his friends and members of his family, one after the other, bringing their dead bodies to the morgue? She recalled how this child's sister, Fatima Sughra, had pleaded with her in Medina to leave him behind with her so that she could pass her days in the company of the child. She remembered how this child, Ali Asgliar, had clung to his sister and would not go to anybody till her lord had come over and whispered something into its ears. What were the words which Hussin had whispered to Ali Asghar in Medina, when he was in his sister's arms, she did not know but she distinctly recollected the child's coming over with a smile from his sister's arms into his fathers' outstretched arms. What a contrast the smiling face of Ali Asghar, barely 6 months old at that time, presented to the attenuated and emaciated face of the child lying in the cradle before her!

Every minute that was passing was increasing the agony of the child and grief of the mother. Umme Rabab did not know what she could do except watch the child dying by inches. She was just getting reconciled to this thought when the child, with one desperate attempt, lifted itself and came into Umme Rabab's ar,s. Though unable to cry through sheer weakness, Ali Asghar uttered a heart-rending moan which tore asunder the helpless mother's heart. She clasped the child to her bosom and stood motionless. She heard a rustling noise behind her and, turning round, she saw Imam Husain entering the tent. Seeing him she could no longer contain herself and rushed towards him saying, "Sire, my innocent son is dying of thirst. For God's sake do something to save him." Imam Husain looked at her and then at the child. He could see how true her apprehensions were. After a moment's thinking he said to her: "Umme Rabab, give Ali Asghar to me. As a last attempt, I shall take him in my arms and appeal to the army of Yazid to give him a few drops of water to save his innocent life." Overjoyed at the thought of her son getting some water, Umme Rabab immediately put Ali Asghar in Imam Husain's arms saying: "Sire, go quickly, for time is most precious for saving my son's life. May God help you in getting some water for him. When you take him out into the scorching sun, do cover him up with your robe, because, in his present condition, he might wither away like a flower in the blaze outside." Husain took the child in his arms, covered him with his robe and went out of the tent. The mother followed him till the exit and stood there watching him go towards the army.

The soliders of Yazid saw Husain coming towards them, his back bent, his body wounded, his beard turned completely white with sorrow and grief in the span of a few hours. They saw him bringing something held under his robe. Many thought that Husain was bringing the Holy Qur'an to plead with them that the conflict between him and Yazid be resolved by the arbitrament of this Holy Book. He walked towards them and stood at a shouting distance and, when he felt that they could see him clearly, he removed his robe which was covering Ali Asghar. He held the child high in his hands and, in a loud and ringing voice, he said: "O soldiers of Kufa and Damascus, I came to this place at the invitation of your people to preach to them the principles of Islam. Instead of treating me and my people as your guests, you betrayed us and denied us even water for the last 3 days. You have killed my loyal friends, my nephews, brothers and son. If in your warped judgment we had commuted a crime, by not bowing to the will of the tyrant Yazid, whom you have accepted as your spiritual lord, my young son, whom I am holding before you, has not committed any sin, because he is just an infant. For the last 3 days he has not had any nourishment — not even water. He is now dying of thirst. Islam is the religion which you profess to follow and, in the name of Islam, I appeal to you to give a little water to my innocent son to save his life. I am sure many of you must be having young children of his age. I implore you, for the love of your children, not to let this child die of thirst." Saying this, he turned to the child in his hands and said: "Ali Asghar, my son, I wish you could tell them to what state your thirst has reduced you." As if in response to this, Ali Asghar opened his mouth and started turning his tongue, which had become bone-dry on his parched lips.

Husain's words and Ali Asghar's mute appeal for water had a magic effect even on the heartless mercenaries who were arrayed against them. Many soldiers recalled the faces of their own children back home lying contentedly in their cradles, well-fed and well-protected. Their paternal instincts for a moment aroused pity in their hearts for this innocent baby. Some of them, in spite of themselves, could not help shedding tears to hide which they had to turn their faces. Some bold ones amongst them were whispering to one another about going over to the Commander of their army, Amr Saad, and asking him to save the child's life by providing some water for him.

Husain was waiting for the reply to his appeal, with the child in his arms. He felt that another appeal to them might he helpful, so he once again addressed the soldiers of Yazid: "Army of Yazid, some amongst you may be thinking that I am asking for water for the child with the intention of satisfying my own thirst and the thirst of other children and ladies in my camp. If you think so, let me tell you that I am incapable of any such ruse. If you do not feel convinced, I am prepared to hand over my son to you, so that you can yourself take him and give him water. I am laying down Ali Asghar on the sand so that any one of you can come and pick him up and return him to me after quenching his thirst." Saying this he spread his robe on the ground and put Ali Asghar on it in full view of the opposite army.

Husain's action had an electrifying effect on many of the soldiers. Some of them felt like going ever to Amr Saad, their Commandar, and telling him that he could not deny a few drops of water to the child when Husain had clearly demonstrated that there was no stratagem to get water for himself.

Amr Saad sensed that, if much time elapsed, some of his soldiers might revolt against him — soldiers who had not hesitated to slaughter young Hashimite boys of 12 and 14, but who were now touched to the quick by the mute appeal of this babe, a few months old, for some drops of water. He turned to his ace archer Hurmula, who was standing beside him, and said: "Hurmula, here is the chance for you to earn the best favour of Yazid. You cut short this agonising situation by your arrow. Demonstrate your skill by piercing the throat of the child."

The heartless archer's greed and cupidity were aroused. He pictured to himself the favours he would gain at the court of Yazid when it would be narrated that he came to the rescue of Amr Saad, when he faced a very delicate situation with many of the young soldiers staging a near revolt on beholding the piteous condition of the hapless and helpless child. Without waiting for a second, he picked up his bow and arrow and took aim at the child. At the same instant Husain picked up the child from the ground. The arrow whizzed past the ground where the child was lying a minute before. Now Ali Asghar was in his father's arms. Seeing that his first arrow had gone waste, Hurmula took out another one and aimed it at the child. An expert marksman though he was, he could not take correct aim as he saw in the distant background near the door of the tent a woman's veiled form. He felt that it must be the mother of the child anxiously and expectantly waiting for the child's return.

The reason for his second arrow missing its mark was that, heartless as he was, he could well realise that, with the piercing of the child's throat, he would be shattering the mother's hopes and heart. Amr Saad, who was watching the two abortive attempts of his best archer, known throughout the kingdom for his expert and unfailing marksmanship, got scared at his failures. He knew fully well that every second that elapsed was dangerous for him. He felt that, what the other bold and brave soldiers on Husain's side could not achieve, might be achieved by this little infant in saving the day for the Imam. He, therefore, exhorted Hurmula with all the persuasion he could command, giving him most extravagant promises of reward, to hasten with his third arrow. Little did the wretch need of these because, feeling humiliated and chagrined at his own weakness, he put the third arrow in the bow and taking aim, let it go. It was released with such uncanny accuracy that it found its exact target. It was too big for its target for, how big is the throat of a child a few months old! The arrow not only pierced the throat of Ali Asghar but tore it asunder and dug itself into Imam Husain's arms. Such was its impact that the child's blood gushed forth as if from a fountain and splashed the face of the father.

Husain clasped the dead body of his infant to his chest and, with tears rolling down his cheeks, muttered: "My innocent son, to what depth of degradation these people have sunk that they could not even spare you".

Husain was hesitating for some time what to do after this. He knew that the child's mother was waiting for him to bring it back to her. What if she asked him whether he had got water for him? If he told her that the enemies had killed him with an arrow, would she not ask whether, before killing him, they had quenched the child's thirst? He went forward a few paces and then retraced them. His second thought was to bury the child there and then and then go and tell the waiting mother about what had happened. But he rejected this idea, because he realised that the mother would like to have a last look at her dead child's face. But then he thought of the agony the mother would feel when she saw the mangled remains of her child.

Steeling his nerves Imam Husain covered the corpse of the child with his robe in the same way as he had covered it when coming to the battle-field and walked towards his camp. As soon as he entered it, he saw the anxious mother wailing impatiently.

She looked at his drooping face smeared with blood and saw tears rolling down his checks. She understood what he had come to tell her. As soon as he saw her, he said: "Umme Rubab, as your husband and lord, I ask you to make one promise to me. This I am asking from you as my last wish." She quietly said: "Sire, I shall do exactly as you want me to. Tell me what they did to my innocent son, tell me all. Other young warriors of the family died fighting bravely but my helpless child was too young for that. Tell me whether they gave him water before killing him. Even animals are given food and water before they are slaughtered."

Husain whispered: "Rubab, I beseech you not to curse the persons who killed your innocent child so mercilessly. Alas, they did not give him a drop of water. My appeal to them for water for him was replied with an arrow." Saying this, he removed the robe from Ali Asghar's corpse and handed it to Umme Rubab.

Husain's sister Zainab, who had come over there on hearing her brother's voice, saw the mother taking the dead child into her hands, clasping it to her bosom, and then collapse with a piercing shriek. She rushed in to hold Umme Rubab. What mother could see her child in that state and still remain calm and patient!

Zainab called all the ladies of the family to come over and console Umme Rubab. Husain stood there for quite some time lost in thought. He was perhaps remembering all that he had lost in the space of a few hours. Not even his innocent child had been spared by the enemy who, it seemed, were bent upon extermirating the family of the Prophet of Islam, though professedly owing allegiance to him.

He must still in thought when Umme Rubab came over to him and said: "Sire, I want my child to be buried by you with your own hands. I know that when you are no more, the enemies will nor hesitate to desecrate the dead bodies of the martyrs. I want this child to be spared such defilement after death."

Husain took the child's dead body from the mother's hands, and walked out of the camp. He dug a little grave with his sword with none to assist him. At such times it is usual for others to attend the burial ceremony but Husain had none with him who could lend him a helping hand, much less bury the child. He placed the child in the grave and covered it with the earth. It is customary to sprinkle some water over the grave but that was not possible when even in its last hour the child could not get a drop to drink.

Husain sat at the grave with his tears rolling down on the grave. After offering Fateha at the grave, Husain raised his head heavenward and prayed: "O God, Thou art my Witness that I have not faltered in my duty to the last and have given sacriices of all my dearest ones, including my last one, this my babe-in-arms."

The Supreme Sacrifice

Husain was atone, all alone with none to befriend him, none to help him, none to defend him. On the other side was an army of several thousand strong, thirsting for his blood. He was sitting on the sand outside his tent listening to the beating of drums of the enemy punctuated by their battle cry: "Is there any person left to come out and fight with us?" Husain wondered whether they were expecting any person to be left or whether their battle cry was just to mock him. Did they nor know that all his loyal friends had died fighting valiantly to defend him? Did they not realise that not a soul was left from his brothers, cousins, nephews, sons and his kindred, each one having laid down his life in the few hours between sunrise and the post-noon period? Now there was left only his son Ali Zainal Abedeen, who was confined to bed with fever which had been raging for days and which had so weakened him that he could hardly lift his head, what to talk, of walking or marching to the battle-field.

The declining sun was now casting lengthening shadows on the plain of Karbala. It seemed that Husain was waiting for the inevitable hour to come. Perhaps he was waiting till the lime for evening prayers so that he could go out into the battle-field after offering his prayers.

The shouts from the enemy's hordes became more and more vociferous. It seemed that now they were clamouring to shed his blood so that, having accomplished their task, they could partake of the feast which their Commander had prepared for them to celebrate their success. Some impatient soldiers came marching towards Husain's camp and shouted: "O Husain, where are your soldiers who were so anxious to protect you and who had sworn to see that no harm came to you so long as any of them lived? Where are your brothers, sons and nephews who had sworn to protect you and to see that nobody raised his voice against yours till any of them breathed?"

Husain was cut to the quick by these taunting words of the enemy. He turned towards the morgue where the dead bodies of his beloved friends and dear ones were lying and, addressing them, he said: "Where are you, Muslim Ibne Ausaja, Zohair Ibne Qain, Habib Ibne Mazahir, Hur Ibne Riyahi and my other faithful friends? Do you hear the taunts of the enemies? Why don't you respond to my last call for help?" Then, turning towards the dead bodies of his nephews and sons, he cried: "Are you hearing me, O Ali Akbar, Qasim, Aun, Muhammad and my brothers? All of you were ever ready to defend me but now I am all alone and without a friend to help me, to defend me, or even to console me in this hour of trial." Turning then in the direction of the river, where the dead body of his dearest brother Abbas was lying, he cried: "Abbas, my brother, are you hearing my cry for help? Why are you not answering me today? From your childhood you were ever ready to chastise anybody who so much as raised his voice against mine, but today, insults and ignominies are being hurled at me. Why don't you come to my help now?" With these words he wept bitterly and added: "Alas, I know that all of you are sleeping the sweet slumber of death — I know that death has created that barrier which you cannot cross to help me."

With faltering step Husain enteted his camp to bid farewell to his sisters, daughters and other ladies of his house. Standing outside his tent he called: "O my sisters Zainab and Umme Kulsum, Umme Laila and Umme Rabab, my daughters Kubra, Rokayya and Sakina and my respected nurse Fizza, come ever to me to hear my Last salutations and farewell message to you all."

His words drew all the ladies of his family who came rushing in and clustered round him. His dearest sister Zainab put her arms round his neck and, looking straight into his eves, said: "My dearest brother, is it true that you are going away for the last time, never to be seen alive again? O brother, has that time come, which l was dreading all day long, for you to depart leaving us at the mercy of these heartless hordes?"

With his head bowed, Husain mattered: "Yes, Zainab the time has come for which your mother had prepared you from your childhood, about which your father had spoken to you on his death-bed. For me this parting is saddest, because I know that your real trials and ordeals will not end but only begin today."

"My own brother," replied Zainab, "I was all along hoping against hope that by sacrificing the lives of my sons, Aun and Muhammad, of Abbas, Qasim and Ali Akbar, your life may be spared. Without you, what will be left in this world for ne to live for? Brother, when you go to heaven, plead with our grandfather to call me to heaven, to spare me the insults and ignominies that now await me."

For a moment Husain could not reply to Zainab's pleadings, for he knew how true what she said was. Controlling his own emotions, after a few seconds, he said, "Zainab, if you will leave this world so soon, who will fulfil the mission, who will accomplish the task which I am leaving unfinished? I am entrusting to your care my orphans and widows and the orphans and widows of all my brave soldiers and my blood relations. It is now for you to lead them, to look after them, to care for them and to console them. I shall die in peace if you promise me that you will be to them what were all their dear ones, whom they have lost today." He paused for a while and added: "And Ziinab, I am particularly commending to your care my son Ali Zainal Abedeen, whom illness has brought to the verge of death, and my beloved daugher Sakina who has never been separated from me even for a day. When she will not see me, she will ask you where I have gone. Console her as best as you can. I remember how she was pleading for water to her uncle Abbas but, ever since his death, she has not uttered a word. When you get water after my death, give it first to her."

With these words Husain seemed to be choked with emotions, but controlling himself he went on: "The enemies know well how dearly Sakina loves me and I love her. To satisfy their vengeance against me, they might beat her up, to torment my soul, and, perhaps, lead her as a captive from the place where my dead body will lie. Zainab, do what you can to spare her these tortures and afflictions."

As Husain was saying this, each word was sinking into Zainab's wounded heart. She was choking with sobs and the only reply she could give to the last commendations of her brother was by nodding of her head.

After a few seconds, Husain continued: "Zainab, I have so much to say to you before my last parting but I have so little time for it. Dearest sister, the enemy will take you all prisoners and they will, perhaps march you through the streets of Kufa and Damascus. They may snatch away your veils and parade you through the bazaars of these cities to add to your agony. They may even tie or chain your hands and feet and mercilessly use the lash and spears to torture you all helpless ladies and children of the Prophet's House. That will be the real hour of trial for you, but Zainab, I implore you by the love you have for me, not to lose your patience. When these tortures are inflicted on you all, you give courage to all the ladies and children with you, and ask them to pray to Ged Almighty for fortitude and patience to bear the ignominies, insults, tortures and torments. Zainab, remember at all times that we, people of the House of the Prophet, must stand firm in the hour of our trial without so much as uttering a curse on our torturers and tormentors."

When Husain stopped after saying this, Zainab looked at him through tears and replied in a low voice: "Husain, I promise you that I shall do exactly according to your last wishes. Dear brother, pray for me that, God may give me the fortitude to suffer boldly and patiently, pray that in my hour of trial I may not be found wanting. My dearest Husain, I promise that I shall do exactly as you want me and shall shoulder the responsibilities which your death will throw on me and show to the world that I am your sister, and daughter of Ali and Fatima, and grand-daughter of the Prophet of Islam."

This bold and brave reply of Zairtab served as a balm to Husain's wounded heart. He blessed her and added: "Your sufferings will last a long time and you all will have to endure imprisonment and incarceration. When you return to Medina after your release from prison, convey my salaams to all my friends who may come to mourn my death. Tell them that my last message to them was that I and my near and dear ones died without a drop of water with consuming thirst. Tell them that, when they drink cool water, they may remember me and my faithful followers and members of my family, and the thirst we endured today."b

All the ladies of the family who were listening to the last wishes of Husain were beside themselves with grief. They were, one and all, crying bitterly. Some whose strength had ebbed away on account of thirst and starvation and the sufferings they had undergone at the loss of their brothers and sons during the day, swooned and fell unconscious on the floor.

"I have not yet concluded what I have to tell you, Zainab," said Husain, after a while, "When you go back to Medina, you tell my beloved daughter, Fatima Sughra, that though I had left her behind on account of her ill-health, I never for a moment forgot her and remembered her till my last hour. Convey my love to her and tell her that fate willed it that our parting in Medina should be for ever. When she will learn from you that so many of her uncles, brothers and cousins left Medina but none returned, she will feel disconsolate. Do whatever you can to console her."

With these words Husain stopped. The brother and sister embraced each other. It was the last embrace of the loving brother and sister who had throughout their lives remained closest and most devoted to each other. It was the parting embrace of a brother and sister who knew that they were never to meet again. Zainab was clinging to Husain as if she did not want to let him go, knowing that he would never come back again. Both were crying their hearts out, the sister at the thought of the imminent martyrdom of her brother and the brother at the thought of the predicament in which he was leaving her and the others of his family, women and children — and his invalid son.

Time was now running out and this thought made Husain tear himself from his sister. He went over to each lady and each child and most affectionately and lovingly he bade them his last farewell. He turned to his aged nurse, Fizza, who had looked after him from his childhood, and kissing her hand he asked her to bless him as she had been blessing him since his childhood. To Fizza Husain was like a son. At the time of Fatima's death she had promised her to remain with him and never to leave him. To fulfil that promise she had accompanied him on this arduous journey, in spite of her advanced age, disregarding the advice of all the elderly ladies of Medina who had tried to dissuade her. This parting was rearing her heart to pieces. Her aged eyes were welling with tears as she hugged him and kissed his throat as she had seen his mother doing when he was a little boy. "Farewell, my son, farewell from your aged nurse. May God be with you in the hour of your-supreme trial," she cried from the depth of her heart and with a shriek she fell down. Her grief-stricken aged heart could not bear this saddest parting.

Turning round Husain saw his dear little daughter standing near him and looking up at his face. She appeared to be speechless and dazed with grief. The sorrow depicted on her innocent face tore Husain's heart. He felt as if all the courage he could summon up would not be sufficient to steel his heart for this occasion and tell Sakina that he was leaving her for ever, leaving her to the mercies of the world that had no kindness for her, leaving her to face the woes which had no parallel, leaving her to a fate which had sufferings in store for her. He picked her up in his arms and imprinted kisses on her cheeks which were wet with tears. Ah! did he know that these same cheeks would receive cruel slaps of the enemy just for crying for her dead father!

Putting Sakina on the ground he hurried towards the tent where his son, Ali Zainal Abedeen was lying on a couch with raging fever. He found him almost unconscious on account of high fever. He bent over him and shook Ali Zainal Abedeen by his shoulder and said: "My son, I have come to bid farewell to you. Ali, my appointed hour is drawing close, so wake up and meet me for the last time."

Ali Zainal Abedeen was aroused from the stupor by these words of his father and he opened his eye. He saw Husain for the first time that day and, such was the change brought about in him by the cruel blows inflicted on him during that evenful day, that for one moment he looked at him speechless and bewildered as if he could not recognise him. He saw his father's body with gaping wounds, his hair snow-white, his back bent. With supreme efforts he sat up on the bed and cried: "Oh God, what have the enemies done to my father!" Looking up at Husain he asked: "Father, what has happened to your faithful friends? What has happened to my uncle Abbas, my brother Ali Akbar, my cousins Qasim, Aun and Muhammad? How is it possible for you to be in this state, if any of them is alive to protect you?"

"My son," replied Husain with a sigh, "all of them have

tasted martyrdom in defending me and the cause of Islam. There is no male member left in this camp except you and I. Now my turn has come to go out and die fighting. My destiny is now beckoning me fast and I have come to bid adieu to you."

Hearing this Ali Zainal Abedeen mustered all the strength that was left in him and rose from his bed and said: "Father, so long as I am alive, you cannot go to meet your death. Let me die fighting as my brothers, cousins and uncles have done."

Husain gently put him on the bed and said: "My son, I command you, as your father and spiritual leader, to remain in bed. Your task is to accompany your aunts, mother and sisters and other ladies in captivity, to march through the streets of Kufa and Damascus, with hands and feet in chains, to suffer insults in the court of the tyrant and undergo imprisonment and to bear all these things with fortitude and patience. Your task is to show to the world that we can bear afflictions and sorrows with unfaltering faith in God and our cause. Your destiny has singled you our to demonstrate for all times that real crusade means showing faith in the hour of trial, when confronted with the most difficult and trying situations. What you will suffer, my son, will be far worse than death, for death would bring relief but you may have to live for years with memories of your cruellest sufferings."

With these words Husain clasped his son to his bosom. The father and son parted for ever. The grief was too much for Ali Zainal Abedeen to hear and he fell down on his couch unconscious. Merciful heaven spared him the agony of seeing his father's departure.

Husain felt that if he delayed his departure any longer, the enemy might rush into the camp en-masse. This he could never suffer as he wanted to save his family from the ignominy of the enemy's looting and pillage so long as he was alive. When he reached the courtyard of his camp, he found his faithful steed waiting impatiently for him. Seeing him, the horse neighed with joy. This mount was Zuljanah, presented to him by his grandfather when he was a young boy and just learning to ride. The aged stallion seemed fully conscious of its master's plight. The sight of Husain, wounded and covered with blood, brought tears into the animal's eyes.

Husain stood before the horse for a moment looking hither and thither. Upto this time, there was not a single occasion when his brother Abbas or his son Ali Akbar, or his nephew Qasim, had not helped him to mount the horse holding the stirrups. Instinctively he looked all round him and exlcaimcd: "Brother Abbas, where are you: Why don't you rush forth to help me mount the horse? My Akbar, my Qasim why don't you come forward to hold the stirrups for me today?"

Zainab, who had come to the courtyard of the camp to see her brother depart, noticed the condition of her brother and realised what his feelings were. She rushed up to him and said: "Husain, if there is nobody to help you today, my brother, Zainab will do this service for you. Let me hold the stirrups for you." Before Husain could say anything, Zainab was holding the stirrups. Husain blessed her and jumped on the horse's back. He urged Zainab to go back into the tent and try to console all the and children whose afflictions on that day knew no bounds. In deference to her brother's wishes, Zainab went back into the tent to perform the duties which, from that hour, had fallen to her lot.

As soon as Zainab had gone back into the tent, Husain spurred Zuljanah to move on. The horse did not respond and stood still as if it was glued to the spot. Husain was surprised at the horse's immobility. He knew that, with him, the horse had suffered wounds whilst going to the battle-field on every occasion a friend or member of the family fell flighting. He knew that, with him and members of his family, the horse had also gone without food and water for 3 days. Still Zuljanah's behaviour seemed inexplicable.

Addressing Zuljanah, Husain softly murmured into its ears: "My companion from childhood and my faithful charger, I know that you are old and weary, seeing and experiencing the events of today. But Zuljanah, this is the last time I am mounting you. Take me to the place where my destiny beckons me. Take me to my journey's end."

The horse appeared to understand what the Imam was saying. Though speechless, it indicated by, bending its head towards the ground, the reason why it had stood motionless. Looking down Husain saw his young daughter Sakina clinging to the herse's hoofs and softly moaning: "Zuljanah, I implore you not to take away my father to the field of battle from which none of my dear ones has returned. Zuljanah, I saw my uncle Abbas ride away and I waited for him to come back with water, but my waiting proved to be in vain. Zuljanah, I know from the talk of my father that he is now going away, going for ever and ever, never to come back again. I beg of you not to take him out, if you do not want to see me as an orphan, with nobody left to love and care for me."

Through lack of food and water and sheer exhaustion Sakina had become so weak that Husain could hear her moaning with great difficulty. She had come up to the horse so quietly that he had not noticed her till he looked down in response to the horses indication by bending of its head. Now he knew why Zuljanah had stood still. He immediately jumped down from the horse's back, picked up Sakina in his arms and sat on the ground. The father and daughter clung to each other as if nothing could part them. Both were choked with sobs; both were crying their hearts our. When Husain could somewhat control his emotions, he softly said to Sakina: "My darling daughter, why did you rush out of the tent? My child, you must now remain with your mother and console her. You know, after the killing of Ali Asglar, how disconsolate your mother has become."

Sakina looked into the eyes of her father and innocently exclaimed: "Father, tell me, are you not going out for the last time, never to return? Are you not leaving your Sakina for ever? O father, how will Sakina live without you? When you brought the dead body of my brother Ali Akbar, I thought that his loss would kill me; but then the thought that you were there to console us and be with us sustained me. When you informed me that my uncle Abbas had gone to heaven and that I would never see him, my heart sank within me; but you consoled me. Tell me father, when you are gone, who will be there to share our grief and sorrow, to speak to us a few words of consolation? With whom shall I be able to share my grief? No, rather I will not let you go. You will never go — for Sakina's sake, you will not go." Saying this, Sakina wept. It was the weeping of a child, an innocent child that knew, in spite of her tender age, what death was; what the pangs of parting — eternal parting, brought about by death — were. She had experienced them, one after the other, on that fateful day.

Husain was stunned by the innocent pleadings of his Sakina whom he loved more than anything in this world. He knew very well what was in store for his beloved Sakina, whom he had brought up with love and affection which was unique. He remembered the day, during the journey to Karbala, when, on hearing the news of the death in Kufa of his emissary and cousin Muslim Ibne Aqil, he had called Muslim's young daughter, who was accompanying him, and, patting her with tender affection, had presented her a pair of earrings similar to the pair he had given to Sakina. At that time Sakina had whispered in his ears whether it was true chat her cousin had lost her father, and her saying that, if she herself lost her father, she would not be able to live without him even for a day. Little did she know at that time that the day on which she would be orphaned would dawn so soon!

With supreme efforts Husain controlled his feelings and, kissing his beloved Sakina again and again, he said to her: "My own Sakina, my clearest child, how shall I explain to you that I must go out to meet my death, as others from our house have done. Child, you are too young to understand what is at stake. How can I explain to you that this day I am fighting the battle for the cause of truth and righteousness and I cannot sacrifice them for the sake of all that I hold dearest to my heart. Sakina, I can only tell you that life is transitory and all that is in existence in this world is to perish sooner or later. Child, by dying today, I am only going before you and you will follow me to heaven which is to be our eternal abode. My Sakina,

God Almighty has so ordained that we must suffer the ordeals for the cause of truth. My child, do not hold me back but with a smile on your innocent lips, say goodbye to me."

As if her father's words had kindled some hope in her young heart, she said: "Father, you say that I will also join you in heaven after some time. Promise me, father, that it will be soon — very soon. Father, promise me that you will remember to plead with God to end my separation from you and to unite me with you in heaven, never to be parted again. If you will promise me, father, I shall let you go." Before Husain could reply to her, she added: "And father, I want you to make me one more promise. When I will not see you, I will find the world and life nothing but misery. Though in death you will not be able to see me in person, promise that you will come to me in my dreams so that I will be able to unburden my heart to you and tell you how I suffered without you. If you will promise me, father, at least I shall have something to look forward to every day. I shall wait for the night to come so that, in my dream, I can talk to you, as I have always done; to kiss you and cling to you as I have done every day." With these words she clung to her father with a choking heart.

Husain's heart was bleeding and the innocent words of Sakina made him weep as he had seldom done in the course of the tragedies he had suffered that day, one after another. He burst out crying and the father and daughter sat there embracing each other — both crying their hearts out with grief unconfined.

Realising that time was now running out and hearing the cries from the enemy's army, calling him to the battle-field,

Husain, with the utmost effort, controlled himself. Kissing Sakina again and again, he said; "My Sakina, my beloved child, I promise you what you are asking for. My darling, you also promise me that you will hear all the sufferings, all the tortures that the enemy will subject you to with courage and fortitude. And Sakina, remember that if you will cry for me too much, your aunt Zainab, who has already suffered so much and who will now be shouldering all the responsibilities after me, will be crushed by your sorrows and weeping."

Sakina murmured softly: "Father, Sakina promises you to face all the sufferings and afflictions silently. My beloved father, I shall do exaclty as you want me to." As if she had remembered something, she softly added: "Father, every night I used to come to you and sleep on your chest. Now that will no more be possible. How I wish I could sleep on your chest for the last time so that I could carry its memories for the rest of my life."

Husain could not find any words to reply to this innocent request. He slept flat on the burning sands of the courtyard and clasped his daughter. Sakina rested her head on her father's chest and lay there crying silently for quite some time. The sobs of Sakina and Husain were punctuating the silence that pervaded the camp. Silently Sakina rose from the Imam's chest, kissed him goodbye and stood near the horse. She saw him mounting the horse and riding away, with a last affectionate glance at her that expressed his deepest love for her. She raised her small hand and reverentially bowed in salutation to him — for the last time.

Seeing her father march out for the last time, Sakina

returned to her mother, Umme Rabab, and rushed into her extended arms. With her head resting on her mother's bosom, she was weeping and her mother was caressing her and stroking her head tenderly. Umme Rabab was so much stunned by the magnitude of her grief that she had become speechless.

Zainab heard her brother riding out of the camp. She could nor contain herself and raising the curtain from the door of the tent, she followed him with her eyes.

Imam Husain rode on straight to the armies arrayed against him on the opposite side. The soldiers of Amr Saad saw Husain coming towards them clad in the Prophet's turban and robe. Facing the army, he addressed in a stentorian, clear and ringing voice which was audible to the enemy hordes: "O soldiers of Yazid, I have come to ask you whether you know who I am. If any of you do not know me, I make it clear that I am the grandson of Prophet Muhammad, whom you acknowledge as the Prophet of Islam. I am the son of the Prophet's daughter Fatima and the Prophet's cousin Ali. I am the last of the five persons about whom the Prophet of Islam spoke time and again to his people. Many of you have seen and heard the Prophet. I ask such of you whether you have not seen the Prophet carrying me, and my brother Hasan, on his shoulders, when we were young children. Have you not heard the Prophet say that I was his beloved child? Have you not seen the Prophet crying with grief when I cried on account of any sorrow or affliction? The Prophet is no more, but I am here before you. You have wounded my heart by mercilessly killing my sons, my brothers, my nephews and my faithful friends, each one of whom was as dear to me as my kith and kin. You have not spared my innocent Ali Asghar, who was too young to cause you any harm. Each of them has been killed by you, hungry and thirsty. You have denied me and my family even food and water, knowing well that the scorching heat of this plain is multiplying our agonies and sufferings. I ask you, in the name of God and His Prophet, what have I done to deserve this treatment?"

With these words Husain paused for a while to get a reply to his question. Amr Saad, (Commander of Yazid's army, replied saying: "Husain, there was no need for you to say what you have said, because we are not going to relent a bit. We have given the choice to you to accept Yazid as your spiritual lord and master, and subject yourself to his rulings and decrees in all matters, spiritual and temporal, recognising him as the Leader of the Fathful and successor of the Prophet. If you want to save your life, and save your family from the sufferings which await them, you surrender to our demand. There is no other choice before you."

Husain heard this reply silently and said: "Amr Saad, your father was a companion of the Prophet and, of all the people, you were a witness to all that I have mentioned, because you were very often accompanying your father when he used to visit the Prophet. Do you expect me, for a moment, to accept Yazid, who is, to your knowledge, a debauch and a profligate, as the spiritual leader of the faithful and rightful successor of the Prophet? Do you expect me to accept all the distortions and changes that he wants to introduce in the tenets of Islam and be a silent spectator just to save my life and to stop the brutal treatment you plan to mete out to my children and ladies?

Let me dispel any doubt that you may be entertaining and make it clear to you that, if you want me to compromise my principles for the sake of worldly gains, I shall never do it. If you want to offer me the choice between honour and death, I shall prefer death. If sacrifice of Islamic principles and Quranic teachings is the price you are demanding for my life and the honour of my family, I am here and now rejecting your offer. I am asking you, in the name of Islam, to tell me whether I have, even in a single instance, acted contrary to the principles of religion? Have I done anything to justify the torments you are inflicting on me? O ye who claim to be the followers of the Prophet, do not smear your hands with my blood for, on the day of reckoning, you will have to face my grandfather and my mother who will ask each of you why you shed my blood, knowing that I was innocent; knowing that I had not done any harm to any of you. O soldiers of Kufa and Damascus, what I have suffered at your hands during the day is enough to kill me, even if you desist from slaughtering me. I appeal to you to think, for God's sake, what you have done and what you are bent upon doing. Even now it is not too late for you to repent. Despite all that you have done, I shall not curse you, for it is the tradition of the Prophet's house to pray for enlightenment of those who torture and torment us; to pray for the forgiveness of these who sincerely repent and who, through contrition, change their future life."

Husain's speech was most eloquent, reminding those who were hearing him of the eloquence of his father when he used to mount the pulpit and address the congregation in the Mosque at Kufa. However, the greed of the mercenaries had complete sway over their hearts and minds. They were thinking that their task was almost accomplished and they would become eligible for the extravagant rewards which they had been promised, if they brought the heads of Husain and his followers to Yazid's court.

Amr Saad noted with satisfaction that his soldiers were still thinking in terms of worldly gains, rather than rewards and retributions of the other world. He saw that they were not prepared to heed the rumbling of a distant drum. This emboldened him and he replied back to the Imam: "Husain, we have heard enough from you. You have not accepted the one and only condition we want you to fulfil, thaa is, explicit allegiance to Yazid as the spiritual mentor with final authority to him to do what he wants in all religious matters. Since you are not accepting this, you will be beheaded, say what you will. We know that, against the over-whelming odds, you have not the least chance but still you are trying to gain time. In your present plight, even the weakest of my soldiers would be more than a match for you, what to talk of the whole army I have got under my command."

These taunting words aroused Husain's wrath. His Hashimite blood was now boiling at the insulting words uttered by Amr Saad. After all he was the son of Ali, the Lion of God, whose victories had become known throughout the length and breadth of Arabia. Had not Ali scattered vast armies of infidels single-handed and saved the day of Islam against overwhelming odds? His ire was aroused and he wanted to show these hirelings and stooges of Yazid that if he wanted, he could give them a taste of his sword, even in that condition.

Trembling with rage, Husain put his hand on his scabbard and unsheathed his sword, which he had inherited from his father. Like a lion he roared: "Amr Said, I accept your challenge and offer single combat to the bravest of the brave in your army. Nay, not one but as many as you want to sent to fight me, one after the other."

The cowardly Commander of Yazid's forces and his equally pusillanimous soldiers were shaken by Husain's words. They recalled how Ali, father of Husain, had dealt with the best warriors of his opponents' armies in the different battles fought by him. None had the courage to accept the gauntlet thrown by Husain and go out for single combat with him.

After hurried consultations with his officers, Amr Saad gave orders to fire a volley of arrows at Husain. He also gave orders to his infantry and cavalry to converge on Husain with swords, scimitars and daggers. Husain, with sword in hand, charged on the attacking soldiers mowing down all who came within the range of his sword. A confusion arose in the enemy ranks, because all the soldiers of Yazid's army were clashing with one another whilst Husain was charging and cutting through their ranks. He first attacked the right wing of the army and the enemy soldiers in utter confusion fell back. He veered round and launched a furious attack on the left wing of the army and, before the soldiers could realise where he was, he had cut through the core of that wing. He then turned like lightning to the centre of the army and the cowardly soldiers, who were anxious to save their lives to get the benefit of the awards for which they had sold their souls, retreated in panic and confusion. Husain's sword was flashing in the blazing sun like lightning. So swift were his movements and so well-trained for battle was his charger that with incredible speed he was able to scatter and mow down the opposing soldiers. The confusion was becoming worse confounded in Yazid's army, because his soldiers who were charging forward, were finding themselves clashing with each other. For a moment in utter panic the soldiers felt as if Ali, the father of Husain, had descended from heaven to fight and defeat the whole army of Yazid. Some of the soldiers were awestruck by the battle prowess shown by Husain, this aged Husain, who had no food and water for 3 days, whose heart was torn by the loss of all his dearest ones and every inch of whose body was covered with wounds. They could not help exclaiming spontaneously their admiration for the bravest fight he was putling up in the face of heaviest odds any warrior had faced in the history of the world. The more cowardly amongst them were piteously appealing io him to spare them — to spare their contemptible lives.

The army that had tried to converge on Husain was now scattered and in full retreat. He halted in his charge to see that the way to the rivulet, the tributary of the Furat, was new clear. He saw the dead body of Abbas lying there. Instinctively he exclaimed: "Abbas, did you see your brother's last fight? My brother, in life you were always ready with praise for any brave deed. Why don't you say 'bravo' to me?"

Husanu looked at the sky and saw that the sun was now declining. He realised that it was time for the evening prayers. He thought that, as the soldiers had fallen back, he could use the respite to offer his evening prayers. With this thought he put hack his sword in the scabbard.

Amr Saad and his soldiers, who were now watching Husain from a distance and conferring amongst themselves about their next move, were surprised to see Husain sheath his sword. Some one said that it was a golden opportunity to attack Husain but none had the courage to march towards him after testing his skill with the sword. Amr Saad ordered his archers to fire volley after volley of arrows, his infantry to hurl stones and missiles at him from a distance. He asked some of them to catapult stones and burning coals it him. The orders were executed without a moment's loss.

Husain, who was already wounded from head to foot, was now receiving one mortal wound after another in quick succession. His blood was flowing so fast that he was finding it difficult to remain on horseback. Dizziness was now overpowering him. He knew that his fight was now over. He felt that his sister Zainab might be near the tent watching him. He wanted to spare her the sight of his death. Putting his arms round his horse's neck he said: "Zuljanah, lake me to a low lying area from where I may not be visible to my family in the camp."

Such was Zuljanah's understanding of his master's wishes that he immediately bolted, carrying Husain to a place which was in a trough. Knowing that Husain was now semi-conscious and not in a position to dismount, it spread out its front legs so that Husain may not fall heavily on the ground but slip easily on to it. Zuljanah was accustomed to this when it used to carry Husain as a child, when he was too young to dismount. Husain managed to slide down from the horseback to the burning ground beneath; but for a few moments his body remained suspended on the spikes of the arrows that had pierced his body from top to toe. He immediately lost his consciousness.

****

From the camp's exit Zainab was watching her borther's last battle, lost in admiration at the brave fight put up by him. She had seen him scattering the enemy's hordes, then halting in his march and finally, the horse riding away very fast to a place from where she could not see him. In a veil covering her from head to foot she rushed out towards a hillock near the camp so that she could have a full view of the battle-field. From this hillock, known ever since as "Zainab's Hillock," she saw her brother lying unconscious on the burning sands and Zuljanah standing guard over him with its head bowed. She was at a loss to understand what was happening there.

Husain was now in a semi-conscious state. In this condition he felt that all the prophets of the bygone ages had come over to witness his ordeals — Adam, Noah, Abraham, Moses and Jesus, and all the other prophets of yore. He saw them retreating one by one, saying to one another that they could not bear to see his helpless and saddest plight. He saw his own grandfather Prophet Muhammad, his father Ali, and his brother Hasan, weeping at his helpless condition. He heard them also say to each other, that they too could not see his suffering and agonies, and leave with limitless grief and sorrow. Then in his sub-conscious state he saw Fatima his mother come over weeping and wailing, and saying: "My Husain, what they have done to you. My child, none of them had any pity for you! Did no one amongst them recognise that you were the Prophet's dearest child ? My Husain, there is nobody to be near you in your last hour, but, my I child, am here to be with you. I will not let your head lie on the burning sands of Karbala. I will hold it in my lap, till the last."

He felt as if she had come near him and put her tender hand on his forehead, much as she used to do during his childhood. On his buring forehead he felt something cool and comforting — he thought it was his mother's hand wiping the blood and sweat from his fore-head.

His senses revived at this sensation and he opened his eyes. He saw the sun directly over him and his horse trying in vain to protect him from its blazing rays. The realisation dawned on him that he had stopped the fight, so that he could finish his evening prayers. He felt that unless he hurried with it, the enemy may not give him time to complete it. There was no water available anywhere for ablution so he cleansed his hands and face with the burning sands of the desert and began his prayers. He finished them and with his head prostrated in prayers, he addressed his Maker: "My Allah, Thou art my Witness that I have fulfilled my mission in life without any hestitation, without squirming, without faltering, without complaining... My Lord and Lord of the Universe, I submit unreservedly to Thy Decree and resign myself to Thy Dispensation."

Whilst he was still offering his prayers, Amr Saad called upon his warriors to cut off Husain's head. They were so cowardly and scared after having tasted his sword that none could muster enough courage to go near him and carry out the Commander's orders. They were willing to wound but afraid to strike. Even Amr Saad's coaxing and cajoling could not instil sufficient courage in them to venture near him. Amr Saad then asked Shimr to go forth and behead Husain wilst he was still engaged in prayers. He offered him highest rewards and, to give him heart, he even offered to accompany him and stand by him, sword in hand. The two to them marched towards the place where Husain was lying, his head still prostrated in prayers, his lips uttering prayers to the Almighty God of the universe.

When the two of them reached the spot, they heard murmurs from Husain's lips. Shimr thought that he might be cursing those who had done everything to exterminate his family and friends, who had so brutally and mercilessly treated him. He bent over the Imam's prostrated body to hear what he was saying, when he caught these words: "O Allah, I beseech Thee with all humility to forgive the trespasses of the erring ones for Thou art the Most Beneficent, the Most Forgiving."

Seeing that Husain had concluded his prayers and fearing that he might get up to defend himself with whatever strength was left in him, Shimr decided to hurry up with his most dastardly act. He mounted on Husain's back and, with the sword he was carrying, he prepared himself to cut off Husain's head. Husain, who was now too weak with the loss of blood to raise his head, turned a little and saw what Shimr was about to do. In a faltering voice, which was audible to Shimr, he said: "O Shimr, I am thirsty. I am thirsty. O Shimr, give me a few drops of water before you accomplish your task."

Zainab, who was watching the events as they were happening before her, saw Amr Saad and Shimr reaching the place where her brother lay. She saw Shimr mount her brother's back with sword in hand. In sheer desperation, as a last attempt to save her brother's life, she rushed forth, her hood trailing behind her. She reached the place where Husain lay and going before Amr Saad, she said: "O Amr Saad, I appeal to you as the grand-daughter of the Prophet of Islam, to save my brother's life." He turned his face away from her and so she went over to the other side and said: "O son of Saad Bin Abi Wakkas, will you stand here and watch my brother being slaughtered so mercilessly without a drop of water? In the name of God, I appeal to you to save Husain's life." He still remained silent as if he was completely oblivious to her pleadings and appeals.

All this was seen by Husain and, great as his agonies and pains were, he could not bear to see his sister being humiliated by the utter disdain of Amr Saad. He also knew what his sister would feel if his head were to be severed in her full view. Mustering all the strength that was left in him, he raised his voice and said to Zainab: "My sister, I appeal to you to return to the camp immediately. For the sake of the love you bear for me, hasten to the tent. It will give greatest pain to me if you remain here any longer."

Zainab rushed back ro rhe camp weeping copiously and lamenting. On reaching the camp she rushed to the tent where her nephew was lying on his sick bed. She shook him up and told him what she had beheld a moment earlier. Supporting him she brought him to the exist of the camp. Both of them stood there silent and speechless. They felt that nature itself was sharing their grief, because a strong gust of wind arose and carried with it the red particles of burning desert sand. It ruffled up the waters of the Furat and an angry murmur arose from the torrents that were flowing by. In the distant, dusty panorama they saw a spear with Husain's head on it. They heard the drums of Yazid's army proclaiming the end of the battle. Zainab with a shriek wailed: "O my brother Husain, my brother Husain! At last they have killed you, they have beheaded you without a drop of water." With these words she fell unconscious into the arms of her nephew. He gently put her down on the floor and, prostrating his head on the ground, exclaimed: "O God, we mortals resign ourselves to Thy will. From Thee we have come and unto Thee shall be our return."

The Night of Tragedy

A thick pall of dust was hanging over the battle-field of Karbala as the sun was setting. The events of that day, the carnage and massacre of saintly souls had cast a gloom on that desert tract. An eerie silence was prevailing which was from time to time broken by the sound of drum-beating to celebrate the victory — the hollow victory achieved by a host of well-fed, well-equipped soldiers against a handful of brave warriors, tormented by three days of thirst and hunger, each of whom had fought every inch of his ground and displayed valiance which has remained unparalleled in the annals of mankind.

When the beating of drums had stopped, the desert wind carried the sound of wailing from tents pitched on a hillock, tents which had been plundered and burnt, tents which had been ransacked, looted and pillaged. These ramshackle tents were the remains of Husain's Camp. The moaning sound that was coming from them was of the ladies and children of the Prophet's house who had suffered untold hardships and indignities at the hands of Yazid's mercenary minions. Not long after the ruthless killing of Husain, Yazid's soldiers had marched on the camp where the defenceless ladies and helpless children of Husain and his devoted followers stayed and, with ruthlessness and savagery which only these barbarians were capable of, had robbed them even of wearing apparel. There was not much that they could lay their hands on. The son of Ali and Fatima was not accustomed to worldly luxuries and what they found in his camp sorely disappointed them. The coarse clothes they could get had only immense sentimental value for the ladies and children who were deprived of them, because many of them had been woven by Fatima with her own hands. The small wooden cradle which they rook away had inestimable value for Ali Asghar's mother, because it had associations with that child who had died a little while ago in his father's arms, with his throat pierced by the arrow of Hurmula.

The widows and orphans who had, during the short space of a few hours, lost all their dear ones were brutally beaten and lashed by the ruthless marauders. Not satisfied with their heartless brutality, the enemy set fire to the tents. What a holocaust it was! A young child was seen rushing out of one of the burning tents with his clothes aflame. One of the enemy soldiers, seeing his pitiable condition, came to his help and put out the flames. The child looked at him with surprise because he had not expected to find even a spark of human feelings in the brutes who had come to inflict tortures on them. Seeing that he was somewhat different from the others, he sobbed: "O Shaikh, when you have been so kind to me, do me one more favour and show me the way to Najaf." The man was very much surprised at this request. He replied "Najaf is far away from here; in fact it is several leagues from here. But tell me, why you want to know the way to Najaf." The child innocently replied: "I want to go to the tomb of my grandfather Ali in Najaf and tell him what your people have done to us — how our men have been butchered; how our ladies have been whipped. I want to tell him how the earrings were snatched away from the ears of Sakina, my cousin, and how she was left bleeding and in pain."

Zainab, who was now in charge of the camp, according to the last wishes of her beloved brother, did not know what to do. Should she ask all the ladies and children to perish in the consuming fire rather than suffer the indignities they were subjected to? Whose counsel and advice she could take in this hour of trial, for, Ali, the ailing son of Husain, was lying unconscious on the bare floor of one of the burning tents? Even the mat on which this young Imam was lying had been snatched away. Zainab had no alternative but to turn to Ali Zainal Abedeen who, though seriously ill, was the only person whose decision in such a crucial matter had to be followed. She rushed to him and shook him hard saying: "O my brother's son, as our Imam I appeal to you to tell us what we should do in the present trying circumstances. Shall we remain in the tents and allow ourselves to be devoured by the fires that are raging or go out of the tents into the open?" He opened his eyes burning with fever. With effort he rose and replied to Zainab, "My aunt, it is our religious duly to do all we can to save our lives. We must all leave the tents and go out into the open, however unpalatable it may he to us." On hearing this Zainab and Kuslum led all the ladies and children out of the burning tents. She helped Ali Zainal Abedeen to go out into the open.

Soon the fires raging in the tents subsided. Only one tent remained though partly damaged by the fire. The ladies and children salvaged whatever they could of their meagre belongings and huddled together in the remnants of that one tent which afforded them some shelter.

With the advent of the night the moon appeared on the horizon. It appeared tinted with red. Whether it was due to the effect of the dust that was hanging heavily in the atmosphere or whether the silver orb was red with anger at the atrocities that were perpetrated on the innocent people of the Prophet's bourse, it is difficult to say. The thirsty children who were still without water, were going out of the tents to open their mouths in vain attempts to catch the dew that was falling in tiny drops. But such was the heat radiated by the sand that even the dew drops were evaporating in the atmosphere.

The base and despicable instincts of Amr Saad and his subordinate officers were not gratified even with the inhuman tortures they had inflicted on the widows and orphans in Husain's camp. They were assembled to consider how they could further satisfy their thirst for revenge. Someone from them suggested that the bodies of the martyrs from Husain's camp may be trampled under the hoofs of horses after they had given a burial to their own dead soldiers. This suggestion led some persons from the tribe of Bani Asad to get up and protest that they would not permit the body of any of Husain's followers from their tribe to be defiled in this manner. Others got up and similarly objected to such treatment being meted out to the corpses of Husain's companioas belonging to their clan or tribe or in any way related to them. Amr Saad seeing the opposition decided that only the body of Husain may be trampled under the feet of horses. For this purpose horses were shod afresh and the brutes carried out their purpose. There was not a soul amongst them to say that, though Husain was not related to him, he was the Prophet's grandson and his blood relationship with the Prophet deserved better consideration, if not in life, at least in death. Not one amongst them had the decency to say that the Prophet of Islam had expressly enjoined on them not to desecrate or defile even the corpses of the fallen foes who had died in battle against the Prophet. When Zainab and Kulsum, the loving sister of Husain came to know that only Husain's body was singled out for this barbarous defilement, their grief and sorrow knew no bounds. But what could they do in their utterly helpless predicament?

The night was progressing slowly, av if time had come to a standstill. Though tired, exhausted and fagged out, Zainab realised that she had to perform the duties which now had devolved on her because the illness of Ali Zainal Abedeen, the only surviving son of Husain, had become aggravated by what he had endured. She called her sister Umme Kulsum to her and told her that they had now to look after the orphaned children, according to Husain's last wishes, in the best manner they could. They both decided that they would first count all the children to see that none of them was lost in the wilderness during the pandemonium that had prevailed as a result of the arson, and after that, they both would, by turn, keep vigil outside the tent.

Zainab called all the children to her and started counting and identifying each of them. They found that one child was missing. To her horror and dismay, Zainab found that Sakina, the beloved daughter of Husain, whom he had particularly requested her to look after, before marching out for the last time, was not there. In the dark night, dimly lit by the pale moon, Zainab and Kulsum srarted the search. In vain they were looking hither and thither bu: no trace of Sakina was found. With every minute of her vain search for Sakina, Zainab's axiety was increasing. She knew not where to look for her. She was shouting: "O Sakina, my darling, tell me where are you? Where shall I look for you in this limitless desert?" The echo of her voice was the only reply she was getting. In utter frustration she turned to the place where the body of Husain lay. Running towards Husain's body she cried: "Husain, my brother, I cannot find Sakina, your own darling child, whom you had left to my care. Tell me, brother, where shall I look for her in this wilderness." As she came near the body, the moon, which had been hiding behind dark clouds came out and lit the surrounding area with its pale beams. She saw Sakina clinging to the dead body of her father and sleeping with her head rested on his chest. For a moment Zainab thought that the child had passed away, being unable to bear the torments she was subjected to since her father's martyrdom. Slowly she came near the child and gently cried: "Sakina, my child, I have come here after searching for you all over this desert." The girl opened her eyes. Even in that dimly lit desert Zainab could see that Sakina's eyes were swollen as if she had cried her heart out embracing the body of her beloved father. She gently picked her up in her arms and said, "Sakina, tell me what made you come here. My child, how could you find your father's beheaded body in this dark night." Innocently the child replied, "O aunt, I was seized by an irresistible desire to tell my father what these people had done to me. I wanted to fell him that his dear Sakina had been robbed of the earrings which he had so lovingly presented. I wanted to tell him that the man had not even cared to take them out but snatched them away, tearing my ear lobes. I wanted to tell him that when I had cried with pain, I had been mercilessly slapped by that beast." The child continued sobbing: "When I left the tent I was running aimlessly in the desert shouting, 'Father, tell me where you are lying. Father, Sakina wants to come to you and tell you about all the sufferings she has endured since you left her!' I felt that the wind brought a moaning cry from this direction, as if my father was replying to me: 'Sakina, my own Sakina, come here, come here.' I came running in this direction and I found my father lying here. Zainab, my aunt, I narrated to him all that I had endured; all that you and everybody else had suffered since our parting with him. My narrating everything to him lightened my hearr and I felt an urge to sleep on his chest, for the last time, as I had been sleeping so often when he was alive. So I kept my head on his chest and slept till you came to awaken me."

With Sakina in her hands, Zainzb returned to the camp. Much as she had felt like remaining there near Husain's body and pouring her full heart before him, as Sakina had done, she could not do so because she was conscious that her sister Umme Kulsum and Sakina's mother were waiting for her and Sakina, with fear and hope. She hurried back to the camp as fast as her tired legs could carry her. On reaching the tent, she put the exhausted child in the mother's arms with a request to put her to sleep. For Zainab there were other duties to perform and to keep a vigil outside. It was not so much a thought of protecting any precious belongings, for, of these there were none; it was with the intention of requesting any possible intruders not to disturb the children, the hungry and thirsty children who were one by one falling into sleep of sheer exhaustion.

She had hardly come out of the tent when she noticed that a group of people were advancing towards the burnt out camp. Their figures were silhouetted by the flame-torches they carried. Zainab was beside herself with rage at the callousness of these intruders who, she thought, would not even permit the children the little rest which sleep afforded them. She hurried towards these persons and, when she was within hearing distance from them, entreated them to go back. "If you have come with the object of looting us," she said, "I can tell you that your people have not left with us any thing of value. Our children have gone to sleep and your vandalism will awaken them. If at all you want anything, come in the morning. We helpless women and children cannot escape from your dutches during the night."

A lady, who was accompanying the batch, replied to her in a very polite tone. Zainab was surprised at the respectful tone in which that lady was addressing her: "My lady, we have not come to take away anything from you, for we know that what you have said is true and there is nothing left with you. We have brought some food and water for your children and the bereaved ladies of your camp."

Nothing could have surprised Zainab more than this reply. The people from Yazid's army, and the lady accompanying them, had now reached Zainab's tent. She could see in the flickering light of the torches they were carrying, that what the lady had said was correct. Some of the men were carrying, on their heads large trays containing bread; others had in their hands pitchers full of water. What emotions this sight of water evoked in Zainab's wounded heart can be better imagined than described. For this water each and every one of her kith and kin, her sons, her nephews, her brothers and Husain had craved till death, but net a drop was given to any of them. She controlled herself and took the lady into the tent.

Try as she would. Zainab could not recognise this lady

who was the only one from the enemy's side to have spoken so kindly and respectfully to her since that evening. So she asked her who she was and what had induced her people to relent by sending food and water. The lady replied: "My lady, I am the widow of Hur, who last night came over to your brother Husain from Yazid's army and died this morning fighting bravely in defence of your brother. My husband was a general in Yazid's army, commanding a thousand soldiers. When some of the soldiers of Amr Saad realised that all of you would perish due to hunger and thirst, and they would not be able to take you before Yazid according to his command, they decided to depute me to carry the food and water for you."

As soon as Zainab heard that her visitor was the widow of that brave warrior who had turned his back on the world with disdain to defend her brother Husain, and laid down his life fighting most gallantly, she offered her condolences to the widow. "O sister," she said, "we are all indebted to your husband for laying down his precious life in defending Husain. He was our guest, but alas! he came to us at a time when we had nothing left to offer him. May God grant you patience to endure your bereavement." Hearing this, Hur's widow replied: "My lady, I know not how I can offer my condolences to you, for you have lost, not one, but 18 members of your family." She brought the trays of bread and water-jugs and placed them before Zainab.

Zainab was reminded of the parting wish of her brother. Just before leaving, he had told her that, if she got water after his death, she should first offer it to Sakina. With a tumbler full of water she went over to where Sakina was sleeping and woke her up saying: "Sakina, my child at last there is water for you. Get up, my child, and wet your parched lips and throat with this refreshing drink."

Sakina gor up from her sleep and looked at her aunt. With child-like innocence she asked: "Dear Aunt, you too have remained thirsty for days. Why did you not drink it first before waking me up." Zainab replied with a lump in her throat: "My child, it is usual to give food and drink to the youngest first. Since you are the youngest here, I have brought it to you." Hearing this, Sakina took the mug filled with water from Zainab's hands and ran out of the tent. Zainab rushed out after her shouting: "Sakina, tell me where you want to go in this dark outside." The child replied: "I am taking the water to my brother Ali Asghar, who is sleeping amongst the dead. Did you not tell me that it is usual to offer such things to the youngest? Ali Asghar is the youngest amongst us. I know he did not get a drop of water, for, when father brought his still body, soaked in blood, from the battle-field, my mother had anxiously asked him whether any of the soldiers of Amr Saad had taken pity on his condition and given him water. Father could not say yes in reply to this question; he could only hang his head down with tears rolling down his cheeks. My mother and I understood that Ali Asghar had died thirsty. I cannot forget how my young brother was turning his dried tongue on his parched lips since this morning. O Aunt Zainab, now that water is available, let me give it to him."

This innocent reply of Sakina brought before the eyes of everybody the scene of that morning, with the child Ali Asghar's tragic quest for water. All of them wept bitterly recalling the memory of that infant who had perished with parched lips. Controlling herself Zainab caught hold of Sakina and said: "Sakina, Ali Asghar has been given water in heaven by your Grandfather and he is no longer thirsty. Let him sleep the eternal sleep of death from which nothing can wake him up. See, your father, your uncle Abbas and your brother Ali Akbar, have not tasted the water from the cool springs of heaven because they would not touch it so long as you, my child, remain thirsty. Drink it, my child, drink it so that those who are waiting in Heaven for you to quench your thirst, may also taste the water of Kausar." Sakina silently took the tumbler from Zainab's hands and drank the water with hot tears rolling down her checks. Was she recalling how her uncle Abbas had gone out to fetch water for her, this same water which was now available to her to drink as much as she wanted, never to return?

All the children were served food and water after waking them up from their tired sleep. Can it be imagined how the ladies of the house of the Prophet partook of the food and water with the memory of their dear ones, dying without any food or wacer, still lingering in their minds and eating up their hearts like cankers? The children were put to sleep again. Zainab asked all the ladies to sleep and undertook to keep a watch outside so that, if any intruders came, she could warn them. In spite of the protestations of the other ladies, Zainab would not agree to sleep and let them keep the watch. "It was my brother's wish that, after him, I should assume all the responsibilities of this caravan of captives. I must fulfil the responsibilities that have now devolved cn me according to his wishes" she said with a tone of finality.

Zainab was now taking rounds of the tent with a half burnt tent-pole in her hands. She was sometimes looking towards the morgue where lay the corpses of all her dear ones, Ali Albar, Qasim, Aun and Muhammad, and others. Sometimes she was looking in the direction of the river where by the body of her brother Abbas. Often she was looking in the direction where by the body of her dearest Husain. She was recalling how her brothers, nephew's and sons had tenderly looked after her from the day she had started from Medina on the ominous journey and what a helpless and hapless state she was finding herself in, when they were all gone for ever. With these thoughts she turned in the direction of Najaf where her father Ali lay buried. To her mind came the memories of the days spent by her in Kufa when her father, as the Khalif, was having his seat in rhat town. With what respect she was treated in rhose days by these very people who had not in the least hesitated to hurl insults and ignominy at her on this day! How they had vied with each ether in attempts to humiliate her? Her head was reeling with these thoughts. She swooned with the grief which had become untenable for her. In her unconscious state she saw one person galloping towards the camp as if he was coming from a long distance and wanted to reach there post-haste. His face was covered by a veil. In her sub-conscious state she felt that he was coming to torment the widows and children and so she shouted at him to halt. In her feverish delirium she entreated him not to disturb the ladies and children who were sleeping. She felt that her requests were not heeded by the rider. Burning with wrath she rushed towards the rider, caught hold of his reins and shouted at him: "O Shaikh, I am supplicating you to turn back and not to disturb us in our present predicament, but you are not listening to me. I am the grand-daughter of the Prophet of Islam and daughter of Ali and Fatima. Have you no regard for the Prophet and his family that you are treating my earnest requests with such scant respect?" In her unconscious state she saw the person on horseback lift the veil from his face. She saw the face of her father Ali, with deep sorrow depicted on it. She heard him burst out into tears and say: "Zainab, I have come to take over from you the duty of guarding the widows and children of my Husain, his kinsmen and companions. O Zainab! what have these forces of evil and oppression done to you all." Zainab felt as if she must unburden her heart to her father. "O Father, how late you have come! Where were you when my Ali Akbar and Qasim, Abbas and others fell in the battle-field? Where were you when your Husain's head was mercilessly severed from his body without giving him a drop of water? Where were you when Ali Asghar's throat was pierced with an arrow? Where were you when Sakina's earrings were snatched away mercilessly and when she was brutally slapped by Shimr? Where were you when Yazid's soldiers snatched away our veils and set fire to our tents?" These outpourings of her heart were shaking her body in convulsions. She regained consciousness to find that she was there alone lying on the desert sand with her clothes wet with the tears flowing from her eyes. The dawn was breaking at that time. She recalled with pain the events of the previous day — how at this time Ali Akbar had given the call for prayers and how the morning prayers were offered in congregation by Husain and his devoted followers! She shook off her tears, did substituted ablution on the sand and began her morning prayers. Her morning prayers finished, she laid down her head in prostration and prayed: "O Allah, give me strength to bear the woes that I have to face. Give me courage to carry on the mission which I have to fulfil. Give me fortitude and patience to bear the insults, ignominies and indignities which are to be inflicted on me — O Thou Who art the Source of all Power and Strength."

The Captives' Caravan

When the sun rose on the morning of the 11th of Muharram, it was dark-red in colour with the dust particles, which were heavily laden in the air. This dark colour indicated as if it had become red with shame at the sight it had beheld the previous day and the sight it expected to behold that morning. It was coming out slowly, as if reluctant to cast its rays on the ghastly scene. It saw a very strange and unusual sight, with ladies and children huddled together outside the shambled remains of burnt tents. With no shelter over their heads, the children were sleeping or rather lying semi-conscious with exhaustion, and the ladies were surrounding them as if they were expectantly awaiting some untoward events to occur. A state of uncertainty was writ large on their faces.

On the other side of this camp, the army was making preparations hurriedly for their departure. Amr Saad had called his officers for consultations with them as to what next step they should take. As a result of these consultations, it was decided that the family of Husain should be led as captives, through Kufa and Damascus, to the court of Yazid. Amr Saad, in consultation with some of the generals of his army, decided to march ahead, to convey ro Yazid the news of what had transpired at Karbala and obtain the rewards which were promised. They felt that Yazid would be very pleased with them if they did their utmost to humiliate and subject the family of Husain to the worst indignities and insults. They were vying with one another to suggest in what form they could be tortured and tormented. Somebody suggested that it would add to their grief and agony if they were made to march by the bodies of their dear ones. Amar Saad fell in with this suggestion. Shimr and Khooli were asked to accompany the caravan of captives and to ensure that they were conducted to Damascus with the utmost despatch and hurry.

When the arrangements were completed, the officers who were appointed to bind the ladies and children hand-and-foot, went over to them. They subjected them to the utmost, brutal treatment and tied chains round their necks, hands and feet. The ladies were put on camel-back without any saddles. The ropes and chains were tied in such a way that they linked the hands of the ladies with the necks of the young children. These arrangements being completed, the caravan was taken from the mortuary, where the dead bodies were lying. Such was the discomfiture and grief of the bereaved ladies and children that, on beholding the corpses of the martyrs, they could not control themselves. Several of them flung themselves from the camel-back, in spite of the ropes and chains that bound them, and threw themselves on the dead bodies of their brothers, sons, uncles and other relations. The guards, who were deputed to accompany them, were ready with the lashes and they mercilssly used them, not sparing even young children, whose only crime was that they could not hear the sight of the dead bodies of their dearest ones strewn all over the place without a sheet, without a shroud, and could not control their grief and sorrow on beholding them.

One by one, all the ladies and children were put on the camel-back. They were not permitted to give vent to their grief and sorrow, or to weep over their dear ones. Ali Zainal Abedeen, who was heavily chained and manacled, was made to follow the caravan on foot, in spite of his suffering from high fever. The heads of the martyrs were carried on spears at the head of the procession.

According to scheduled plan, this caravan marched on rapidly towards Kufa. The plight of the captives was such that, if any child fell from the camel-back, the rope that tied it and the hand of some lady became taut, resulting in her toppling over from the camcl-back. The soldiers who were accompanying them would immediately rush towards the child and the lady and use the lash before putting them back on the back of camels.

Within a few hours, with rapid marches, the caravan reached the outskirts of Kufa. Shimr and Khooli, who were the leaders of this caravan, held hurried consultations amongst themselves. They decided that the caravan should be stopped at the gates of the city and a courier should be sent to the Governor, to inform him about their arrival.

When Zainab and Kulsum saw the walls of Kufa, they were reminded of the period when they had stayed in this very city for full four years, during the time of their father. Their father, at that time, was the ruler of the Islamic countries, the Leader of the Faithful, and recognised as the successor of the Prophet. At that time all the ladies of Kufa were vying with one another to secure the favour of Zainab and Kulsum, to invite them to their homes, to secure their blessings for the children. On every auspicious occasion, they used to be invited with the utmost respect and reverence. Now Zainab and Kulsum wondered what treatment they would get in this same city, where they had enjoyed the highest respect and honour; whether the ladies and children of Kufa would remember them; whether they would extend to them any sympathy in their sorrow and bereavement. On second thought they realised that this city had betrayed their cousin, Muslim Ibne Aqil, when he had gone over there as Imam Husain's emissary and it would be futile for them to expect any consideration, any sympathy, any regard or respect from the people of this city, who had acquired a notoriety for the fickleness of their mind and who had become known as time-servers.

Very soon the courier, who had been sent to the court of Obeidullah Ibne Ziad, returned with the message of the Governor, saying that all the preparations had been made and the captives should be marched through the main bazaars of the city. On receiving this order, the caravan marched on. The captives saw throngs of people standing on both sides of the roads. Ladies and children were standing in balconies and windows, to have a glimpse of the captives. The town-crier was heading the caravan, to announce: "O people of Kufa, we are bringing to you Zainab and Kulsum, grand-daughters of the Prophet and the other ladies and children of the family of Husain, son of Ali. To those of you who do not know, we advise that Husain, who had risen against Yazid and refused to recognise his authority as the rightful Khalif of the Muslims, has been defeated and killed with his followers on the battle-field of Karbala. The members of his family are now being taken to the court of Yazid, to face whatever punishment he wants to inflict on them. People of Kufa, this is the fate that awaits all those who question the authority of Yazid, and no person, who tries to raise his finger against the Khalif, will be spared."

Many of the listeners, who had gathered there, were thunderstruck by this announcement. There were not a few who recalled all the kindness that they had received from Zainab and Kulsum. They recollected that in times of their troubles and distress they had sought help from them and had willingly received it. They were surprised to see their plight; to see how miserable they were. They could well imagine their sufferings from their gaunt faces which bore marks of privations and afflictions. Many of them were crying on beholding their grief and sufferings but few had the courage to raise their voice against the forces of tyranny for fear that a similar fate may befall them.

When the caravan reached the main bazaar, there was such a big crowd that it became difficult to make way through it to the court of Obeidullah Ibne Ziad. The caravan halted for some time. It was almost noon and the sun was blazing with all its fury. The children of the Prophet's house, who had not had water during their march from Karbala to Kufa, were feeling extremely thirsty, not to talk of the pangs of hunger they were suffering. Many of them were crying with thirst and hunger. During this halt, the soldiers of Yazid, who were accompanying them, were partaking of food and water which they were carrying with them, and relaxing in the shade. Sakina was repeatedly asking her aunt Zainab for a little water; but Zainab knew that it was useless to request the guards for any mercy, or even for a drop of water. She had full recollection of the heartlessness of these very soldiers who had, till the end, denied even a drop of water to each member of her family — even to Ali Asghar, till his last breath. She recollected how her brother had been slaughtered asking for just one sip of water.

Seeing the plight of Sakina, a lady who was standing in her balcony, rushed down from her house with a cup of water. Breaking the cordon which had been formed by the soldiers, she went to Sakina and offered to her a tumbler of cool water she had in her hand. With gratitude, Sakina took it from her and wanted to drink it; but the lady, looking up at her, said, "I know that you are extremely thirsty and you appear to have suffered terribly. Before you drink this water, I request you to pray to God that He may protect my children from a fate such as has befallen you and the members of your faintly. Pray to God that my children may not be subjected to such miseries and tortures as you are suffering today."

Sakina complied with the request of the lady and she prayed to God, as she was asked by the lady to do. However, the words of the lady recalled to her the stark reality of her miserable plight. She remembered how, not so long before, her every wish was being complied with, with the utmost promptitude; how her every word was taken as a command. She could not help shedding tears at what she had lost, what she had suffered and what she was still suffering. For some time she held the cup of water without drinking, because she could not control her sobs.

Zainab was seeing this and wondering about who the lady was, who had so kindly brought water for Sakina. She had heard the request of the lady, which had brought back memories of her father to Sakina. She thought that she could recollect the face of this lady, though two decades had elapsed since her leaving Kufa. With a little effort, she recalled that this lady was Umme Ayman, who had been visiting her so often when she was staying in Kufa, who was so much devoted to her and had always shown affection for her. She wondered whether Umme Ayman would recognise her. She had heard the town-crier announcing to the public their identity. Could it be possible that Umme Ayman had not heard the announcement and was not aware of it? To remove this doubt, Zainab turned to her and said, "Umme Ayman, I am thankful to you for your kind gesture to Sakina. May God bless you for the kindness you have extended to the bereaved family of the Prophet."

Umme Ayman looked at her with bewilderment. Apparently she had not heard the announcement about who the captives were. She looked hard at Zainab's face, but it seemed that she could not recognise her. Zainab had covered her face with her hair, because her veil had been snatched away. Even if she had net covered her face, such were her sufferings that she was looking several years older than her real age. The dust of the road had covered her face. Starvation and miseries suffered by her had brought such a change in her that a person seeing her after a few days could hardly have recognised her, much less a person who had seen her 20 years before. Umme Ayman, not recognising her, exclaimed in surprise, "Lady, I do not understand why you arc referring to the Prophet's family. For aught I know, the Prophet's family consists of my Lord Imam Husain and his sisters, Zainab and Umme Kulsum, who, May God bless them, are in Medina. What you captives have got to do with my ladies, whom I had the honour to serve and meet, whom I am always remembering in my prayers, and whom I am longing to meet again."

Zainab could see that Umme Ayman had not been able to recognise her. She brushed aside her hair from her face and looking her full in the face, she said, "Umme Aynun, I am Zainab whom you are referring to and here is my sister Umme Kulsum. We are the grand-daughters of the Prophet, the same Zainab and Kuslum whom you want to meet. In what condition you are seeing and meeting us that you cannot even make out who we are! My brother Husain and our other brothers, nephews and sons were killed in Karbala by the soldiers of Yazid. If you will look ahead, you will see the head of your Imam raised on the spear."

When Umme Ayman heard Zainab say this, she turned in the direction indicated by her and saw on the spears several heads. One of them, she noticed, was turned in their direction. From the nobility depicted on the faces of the martyrs she could understand that they could belong to no other family than the family of the Prophet. She again looked hard at Zainab and her sister and recognition dawned on her. Flinging herself down at her feet, she cried, "My Lady, accept my sincerest apologies for what I have said. I could not recognise you. My God, what have the people, professing the religion of Islam, done to you! I could not in my wildest dreams imagine that they would subject you to such tortures, to reduce you to such a state!" Umme Ayman was crying bitterly. She was holding the feet of Zainab and kissing them out of reverence.

The guards who were accompanying the captives saw this and feared that this display of respect and reverence for the Prophet's family might inspire others to come forward and befriend the cause of the captives. They rushed towards Umme Ayman with the whip. She was mercilessly whipped and thrown aside. The caravan was asked to proceed further immediately.

Wending its way through the narrow streets of Kufa, the captives reached the court of Obeidullah. The Governor was seated on a throne and holding his court. The captives were asked to march into the court.

When Zainab and Kulsum were brought before Obeidullah Ibne Ziad, he ordered Husain's head to be placed on a salver and put at his feet. He asked Shimr to identify each member of Husain's family, because he could hardly believe, seeing their faces, that they could be the same Zainab and Kulsum, about whose dignity and bearing he had heard so much. He even mockingly remarked that his first impression was that some slave girls had been brought before him instead of the granddaughters of the Prophet.

Zainab, who was trying to control herself all along and silently suffer the insults that were being hurled at her, according to the promise given by her to her brother at the time of his departure in Karabla, for once lost her temper. Addressing Obeidullah Ibne Ziad, she said: "O son of Ziad, we are the sisters of Husain, and grand-daughters of Muhammed (s.a.w.) whom you acknowledge as your Prophet. You and the other henchmen of Yazid have, for the sake of worldly gains, flouted all the principles of Islam, have desecrated the dead bodies of the martyrs, despite the fact that it is strictly forbidden by religion, and subjected us to the worst kind of ill-treatment, although the Prophet had enjoined on all the believers to treat the captives and, particularly women and children, with sympathy and consideration.

Today you are gloating over your success and rejoicing; today you are thinking that you can insult and humiliate us to your heart's content because there is nobody to say a word to you on our behalf, because you see us in this helpless condition, with none to befriend us, none to protest against the treatment you are meting out to us. But O tyrant, let me warn you that you will find your success ephemeral and very soon the Warth of God will descend on you and those whose cause you are espousing. Very soon nemesis will overtake you and the others who have ruthlessly killed my brother and all the members of our family without the least justification, without the least compunction, simply because they stood steadfast in their belief; because they refused to surrender their principles or compromise their ideals; because they refused to accept Yazid, whose stooge you are, as the spiritual leader of the Muslims on account of his being a known profligate, who has flouted all principles of Islam, trampled under foot all ethical concepts and reduced all human beings to an abject stare."

Obeidullah Ibne Ziad was stunned by this bold address of Zainab. He had never thought that she would dare to speak out so boldly in the helpless condition she was in. He had thought that she would be terrorised by the awe-inspiring atmosphere of his court, particularly at a time when she had suffered such calamities and cruel blows and undergone so much hardships. Not only he but all the courtiers who were present in his court became speechless and listened with rapt attention to her peroration. After a while, he looked round him to see the effect which her speech had produced on those present in the court. He could see tlvat everyone listening to her was hearing every word she was uttering with rapt attention. From the look on their faces, he could discern that they could not help admiring her wonderful courage in speaking out the truth in spite of her helpless position. He thought that many must be comparing her plain and forthright speech with the addresses of her illustrious father delivered to vast congregations from the pulpit in the mosque of Kufa. For a moment he got seared that, if she continued to speak in this vein, she might be able to sway the masses. He tried to stop her by shouting at the top of his voice and ordering her to hold her tongue and threatened to visit the worst kind of punishment imaginable on her and the other captives if she failed to hold her silence.

If Obeidullah Ibne Ziad had counted on silencing Zainab by violence, he found himself mistaken. Undaunted by such threats, Zninab continued to speak with vehemence. She recapitulated how her brother and the other members of her family had dissociated themselves from all power politics and devoted their lives to the service of mankind; to helping the poor and downtrodden people; to befriending the widows and orphans. She contrasted their ways of living with the living of Yazid and his henchmen, how the latter had abandoned all sense of decency and indulged in vices which would disgrace even the meanest of mankind; how Yazid had by his utter disregard of all sense of decency, in spite of claiming to be the "Leader of the Faithful," cast a slur on Islam itself; how his preaching's and precepts had demoralised all those who were looking to him as their king, and spiritual leader. She eloquently narrated the inhuman atrocities perpetrated by Yazid's forces in Karbala and how they had abandoned all humanitarian principles and sense of decency. Her words were sinking into the minds of all who were present there and, through most of them had sold their souls for a mess of pottage, they could not help admitting to themselves that every word of what she had said was fully justified. Several of those present in court were moved to tears. One of the aged companions of the Prophet, Zaid bin Arkan who was blind, rose to admonish Obeidullah Ibne Ziad for subjecting the Prophet's family to such indignities.

It did not take Obeidullah Ibne Ziad very long to assess the situation. Cunning and crafty as he was, he realised that if he did not get rid of the prisoners from Kufa, there might be an uprising against him. He shouted down the companion of the Prophet and ordered him to be removed from the court. He rose from the throne on which he was sitting and hurriedly dismissed the court. He ordered Shimr and Khooli to take the prisoners post-haste to Damascus before they had any opportunity to address the public of Kufa. Both these servile minions were quite relieved to receive these orders, because they too had sensed the danger that lay ahead if Zainab got an opportunity to speak out. After hurried consultations, they decided to immediately take the prisoners out of Kufa and to rake the least frequented roads to Damascus, so that they many not have to face any surprise attack or ambush, if any persons knowing about the tragedy of Karbala took upon themselves to avenge the martyrs.

The captives' caravan marched on and on through the deserts of Mesopotamia. The guards were instructed to let loose their worst vengeance on the helpless ladies and children and the ailing Imam, Ali Zainal Abedeen, who was following the caravan on foot. Due to sheer exhaustion, he used to fall down at every few steps, because a heavy chain was put round his neck and feet, which made marching at a brisk pace most difficult for him, particularly in the condition he was. Every time he stumbled and fell, some brute would jump down from his horse and mercilessly whip him.

During tins march, Sakina fell down from the camel's back. Zainab, who was riding on the camel next to hers, raised an alarm, but the soldiers did not pay any heed ro her. She did not know what to do in her desperate state, for she knew that, if Sakina, who had fainted on falling down from the camel, was abandoned in the desert, she would perish without any food or water, without any succour. In her desperation she turned towards the spear in front of the caravan on which her brother's head was elevated, and cried, "Brother Husain, you had asked me to look after your beloved Sakina after you, but see in what a helpless condition I am. Your Sakina has fallen down from the camel-back and there is nothing that I can do to help her." After saying this, she silently offered prayers for the safety of the darling child. Such was her boundless faith in God that she knew that her prayers would not go in vain and something would happen to save Sakina.

The caravan had hardly gone a few steps ahead when the spear on which Khooli was carrying the head of Husain fell down from his hand and got planted on the gound. Khooli jumped down from this horse to uproot the spear but, try as he would, he did not succeed in plucking out the spear. It remained stuck in the ground as if it had been firmly cemented there. Khooli was at his wit's end as to what he should do about it. He knew that, if the other guards saw this strange phenomenon, they might get terrified and even desert their posts. Quiety he went over to Shimr and whispered into Shimr's ears what had happened. The warped mind of Shimr had a solution for Khooli's problem. He went over to Ali Zainal Abedeen, with the lash in his hands, and demanded to know what was responsible for the spear getting so firmly planted that it could not be moved from its place even by a strong and sturdy man like Khooli, whose physical strength was the only quality he possessed. Ali Zainal Abedeen looked up at his father's head. He thought he saw some tears trickling down the cheeks on the top of the spear. He looked in the direction of his aunt Zainab. She caught his eye and shouted to him that Sakina had toppled over from the bare-back of the camel and, in spite of her entreaties to the guards to pick her up, they had paid no heed to her. Shimr immediately ran back and picked up the child lying unconscious due to the heavy fall and the injuries she had sustained on account of it. As soon as Sakina was put in the arms of Zainab, Khooli was able to lift the spear from the ground. The caravan resumed the march, as if nothing had happened.

The march through the Syrian desert, with the prickly thorns strewn all over, was a cruel ordeal for Ali Zainal Abedeen, who was made to run with the camels on his bare feet. At night the caravan used to halt for a few hours, when the guards used to indulge in feasting and merry-making, giving the least possible food and water to the prisoners — barely enough to sustain them.

One night, they rested in the mountain-top hermitage of a recluse, who had devoted his life to prayers and meditation. Shimr gave the heads of the martyrs to him for safe keeping. Just one look at the face of Imam Husain convinced the hermit that it was the head of a saint. He took it with him and keeping it near his bed, retired to sleep. At night he dreamt that all the Prophets and angels had descended from heaven to keep a watch over the head. He woke up from his sleep, startled and baffled as to what he should do. He decided to ask the leader of the guard about the identity of the persons whom they had beheaded and whose family they had taken prisoners. Rushing out of the monastery, he woke up Shimr and demanded to know who the martyrs were. When Shimr told him that the grandson of Prophet Muhammad (s.a.w.), who had defied the authority of the ruler Yazid Ibn Muawiah, and refused to acknowledge his spiritual suzerainty, had been killed by the army of Yazid and they were carrying the heads of all the persons who had been killed in Karbala, the hermit was shocked beyond words. Recovering himself, he said: "You cursed people, do you realise that you have committed the most heinous crime by beheading your own Prophet's grandson, who undoubtedly was a great saint. Fie upon you, coward, that not satisfied with what you have done, you are so brutally treating his innocent ladies and children and subjecting them to such atrocities!"

These words of the hermit enraged Shimr, who had even otherwise lost his temper with him for waking him up from sleep in the dead of night. With one sweep of his sword, he chopped of the hermit's head. This brute had little regard for the Prophet's injunctions and orders, granting fullest protection to those who had retired from the world and dedicated their lives to prayers and penance. When the life of the Prophet's own grandson was not spared by this brute, what regard he could be expected to have for the commands of the Prophet?

With hurried marches the captives' caravan reached the city of Damascus. On reaching the gates of the fortress surrounding the city, the caravan was halted and a courier was sent to inform Yazid about their arrival and to seek his permission to lead the captives to the court. For one full hour, in the blazing heat of the sun, the ladies and children were made to wait near the door of the city with throngs of people coming over to see them from close quarters. Many of them did not know who they were. They had a faint idea that some prince had risen against the authority of Yazid and had been defeated in a skirmish with the forces of Yazid. They were told that all the dependants of the prince had been taken prisoners and were being taken before the Khalif to receive whatever chastisement he considered necessary for them in keeping with the gravity of their leader's crime against the ruler and his undisputed authority. It appeared that Yazid, who had received a discreet hint from Obeidullah Ibne Ziad about the scene in his court at Kufa, was afraid to make known the identity of the prisoners in Damascus, although he and his father had complete sway over the people for at least a quarter of a century. In hurried consultations with his confidants, Yazid had decided that, till the prisoners were brought into his court, their identity should not be disclosed. He ordered that an announcement he made that a rebel agaiast his authority had been defeated by his unconquerable armies and, to set an example to others, he had ordered the heads of the rebels to be brought to his court with their family. He had proclaimed that day to be observed as a day of rejoicing, to celebrate his victory. He had decreed that his court, the bazaars and the streets and every nook and corner of the city, should be gaily decorated to celebrate this day with full pomp and regalia befitting the occasion.

Whilst the city was assuming a festive look, whilst all the lanes and by-lanes were being decorated with festoons and buntings, the poor victims were suffering under the scorching sun, without, any food or water. The children were crying with hunger and thirst. Some of the ladies from the onlookers were, out of compunction, without knowing to what family these children belonged, throwing sacrificial dry-dates towards them for the well being of their own young children and to ward off all evil from their own dear ones, according to the custom of those days. The hungry children were catching these dates thrown towards them to satisfy their hunger but Zainab and Umne Kulsum were asking them to throw them away. They were telling ihe children that the Prophet had forbidden his family to eat any such sacrificial offerings and asking them to suffer hunger rather than go against the Prophet's orders. They were requesting the ladies not to throw such offerings towards the children because they were from the Prophet's family. Many of the bystanders were baffled to hear these words of Zainab and Umme Kulsum, because they had no inkling about the identity of the prisoners. Many of the ladies were looking on with gaping mouths at Zainab and Umme Kulsum, who had covered their faces with their long tresses in the absence of veils. The ladies of Damascus were whispering to one another whether it could be true that the prisoners were from the Prophet's family. They could not help seeing the remarkable nobility stamped on the faces of the prisoners. Though their faces and bodies were smeared with the dust and desert sand, there could be little doubt that they were from some princely family, from some noble stock.

After a wait of one full hour, orders came from the court of Yazid to bring in the prisoners. All the preparations were made in the mean while to summon the courtiers and ambassadors of foreign countries to the lavishly decorated court. When the prisoners were led into the court, Yazid was seated on an elevated throne, lavishly decorated with gold, and had seven hundred gilded chairs around him, wherein were seated his nobility and foreign emissaries. Yazid ordered the head of Husain to be placed in a gold salver and put at his feet.

When the prisoners were brought before Yazid, he could not for a minute believe that those before him in tattered rags, covered with dust and blood oozing out from the lash wounds and the cuts in the flesh from tightly tied ropes handcuffs and chains could be the grandchildren of the Prophet. He was quite drunk at that time and, without caring to look at their faces, he flew into a rage and bawled out: "Amar Saad, these are not the sisters and daughters of Husain and members of his family. Are you trying to cheat me by letting them get away and substituting in their place some slaves." He was quivering with rage as he said this and his eyes were blood-shot.

Amar Saad, who was present in the court and conjuring up dreams of the rewards his master would bestow on him for accomplishing the task entrusted to him, was scared out of his wits. He knew that Yazid had the habit of acting first and thinking thereafter. Particularly this trait in him was accentuated when he was drunk and he could see that, on this occasion, Yazid was far from sober. Flinging himself abjectly at Yazid's feet, Amar Saad mumbled: "Mercy, O Commander of the faithful. Your humble slave has done exactly according to your august command and the prisoners you behold are Zainab and Umme Kulsum, grand-daughters of the Prophet of Islam, and sisters of Husain. The young girls you behold are Sakina and Rokayya, daughters of Husain. The other ladies beore you are Umme Laila and Umme Rabab the widows of Husain and the others are orphans and widows of Husain's friends and relations. And there before you is Husain's ailing son, Ali Zainal Abedeen."

Saying this, he raised his head a little from the ground to see the reaction on his master's face. Yazid had now focussed his eyes on the ladies whose names Amar Saad had mentioned. He saw that all of them had completely covered their faces with their tresses. In particular he noticed that one lady was standing behind an aged woman from the prisoners, as if she was being shielded from Yazid's gaze.

"Ah, there," he bawled out, pointing in the direction of the lady who had been screened off by the aged maid, "who is that one who is trying to seek shelter behind the old woman and why?" Amar Saad, rising to his feet, bowed abjectly and said, "Your Majesty, she is Zainab, daughter of Ali and Fatima and the old woman standing in front of her is Fizza, the Abyssinian princess, who takes pride in calling hereself the slave of Fatima, and Zainab."

"I shall not let any one protect my prisoners before me," shouted Yazid in a rage. He asked Shimr, who was standing guard over the prisoners, to throw aside Fizza, so that he could have a full view of Zainab.

Seeing Shimr advance towards her, Fizza turned to the Abyssinian slaves, who were standing behind Yazid's throne with bare swords as his bodyguards, and said: "O brothers from my native land, what has happened to your fraternal and communal feelings that you silently watch an aged lady from your country being molested in this manner? With your drawn swords, can't you offer protection to your aged princess from the lashes of this tyrant, who has been our tormentor throughout the march from Karbala to Damascus?"

Hearing these words of Fizza, some of the slaves stepped forward and, addressing Yazid, one of the them said: "Your Majesty, ask Shimr to hold his hands and not to use the lash on our princess Fizza. If he does anything to her, today blood will flow like water in your court."

Yazid was flabberghasted at this affront of his slaves. Drunk though he was, he had sense enough to realise that they were serious and meant what they said. The coward in him panicked at the sight of the bare swords glistening in the light of the chandeliers. He immediately shrieked a command to Shimr: "Stay where you are, Shimr, and do not budge an inch otherwise I shall have your head chopped off." Then turning to the slaves with a wry smile, he said: "My good fellows, I know you are all so devoted and faithful to me and always ready to protect and guard me. I shall not allow anything to be done to touch your sense of honour."

Yazid knew that the scene created by the slaves had humiliated him in the eves of his courtiers and even the foreign emissaries. To show off his triumph and wreak vengeance for his humiliation, he took up the cane with a gold knob lying by his side, and started beating Husain's head with it. Using the cane on the lips and teeth of Husain, he shouted: "Ah, were not these lips receiving the kisses of Muhammad? How delighted would be my forebears to see that I have avenged them for the defeats they suffered in the battles of Badr and Hunayn at the hands of Muhammad? How happy their souls must be today to see that I, Yazid, have taken revenge for their defeats from Muhammad's grandson and his family!" He was chuckling with glee and drinking goblet after goblet of wine, which was making him more and more inebriated. All the ladies of Husain's family and Ali Zainal Abedeen were standing there weeping silently.

Whilst he was still busy with satisfying his vengeance, the ambassador of one of the foreign countries, whose name was Abdul Wahab, felt disgusted at the callousness and brutality of Yazid. He could not bear the sight any more and rising from his seat, he said to Yazid "O King, I would like to know who was the person whose head you are having at the foot of your throne and whose lips you arc hitting with your cane. What heinous crimes he had committed that you are treating him like this, even after death, and subjecting the ladies of his family to such harsh treatment?"

Wine had by now gone so much to the head of Yazid that he became boastful of his achievements. He told the ambassador of the foreign country that he had put to sword all the members of the family of the Prophet of Islam for not accepting and acknowledging him as the Khalif and spiritual leader of the Muslims. He added that he had all the ladies of the Prophet's house before him as his captives and he would subject them to such punishment as the world had not witnessed before, so as to serve as an example to all people who might be having even the faintest idea to challenge and question his authority and sovereignity to deter all such persons from raising their voices against him.

Abdul Wahab, who was a man of learning and culture and who had heard a lot about the Prophet and his descendants and the nobility and piety of their lives, was surprised and shocked to hear this from Yazid. He could not help feeling the deepest admiration for Husain, who had defied the tyrant and refused to sell his conscience even though he had to suffer such a cruel fate. For once he forgot all diplomacy and protocol and said to Yazid: "O King, you have committed the greatest crime, not only against your own religion but also against humanity, by brutally massacring the God-fearing grandson of the Prophet of Islam and the male members of his family and taking as prisoners the ladies and children of his house."

This bold rebuke took Yazid aback, as he had least expected it. Before he could say anything, the ambassador continued: "My people are giving to me the highest respect and honour because I happen to be a descendant of one of their prophets. You lack all sense of decency to have so brutally butchered your own Prophet's grandson who, for aught I know, was so clearly loved by him."

Abdul Wahab then turned in the direction of Ali Zainal Abedeen and said: "Ali, from what I have seen and heard today I am convinced that your father was the boldest soul on earth to put up a fight against the forces of tyranny, oppression and injustice, as embodied in this usurper. Here and now I declare my faith in the religion, to defend whose principles your noble father sacrificed his all, and I want you, as the only true believer in this assembly of men, to bear witness to this fact. I do not care for the consequences of proclaiming my faith and denouncing the errant usurper, who is seated here on the throne and who is the very embodiment and incarnation of the worst qualities in mankind and an epitome of all that is evil."

Hardly he had finished saying this, when Yazid, now mad with rage and smarting under the insults and exposure, such as he had never exacted, shouted a command to his guards to drag away the ambassador and to chop off his head. His orders were carried out by his bodyguards immediately.

A pin-drop silence descended on the court. All the courtiers were stunned by the boldness of the foreigner who had spoken out the truth, in spite of knowing the dire consequences that would follow. Many of them admitted in their heart of hearts the truth of all that he had said and contrasted their own pusillanimity with his courage.

During this time, Yazid was gulping down cup after cup of wine to soothe his frayed nerves. Everybody was waiting anxiously to see on whom he would wreak his vengeance for the insults he had suffered in open court. They had not long to wait, for the tyrant, turning in the direction of Ali Zainal Abedeen, shouted "You, there! You were responsible for the insults which that wretch hurled at me and I shall make you pay dearly for aiding and abetting him for encouraging him to denounce me and praise your father." He paused for a while as if his intoxicated head was muddled and confused in conjuring up what worst punishment he could inflict on Ali Zainal Abedeen.

After a few seconds, he contained: "I shall get your head cut off here and now, in full view of everybody — before your mother, sisters and aunts and before all who are assembled here." Then, as if on second thought, he added: "No, No, killing you will not be enough. I shall torture you to death so that you will die by inches. I shall subject you to such tortures the like of which the world must not have seen, so that your life will become a living death, so that every day, every hour, every minute, you will yearn and pine for death to relieve you of all your sufferings."

As if this diabolical thought of devising cruellest tortures had soothed his sadistic mind, he burst into a loud, hoarse laughter. It was the hysterical laughter of a drunken demon who had no control over his nervous system.

At this stage, Ali Zainal Abedeen in a feeble but clear, ringing voice said: "Yazid, the tortures and ignominies which you have so far inflicted on me can never be surpassed by anything that your crooked mind can think up. For me the worst possible torture has been my standing here with my mother and sisters, with my aunts and cousins, without any veils to cover their heads and faces. Do not for a moment think that I am scared or frightened by your threats. We, descendants of the Holy Prophet of Islam, peace be on him, have been trained from our childhood to face afflictions and sufferings. We know that those who are loved by God are tried by Him and if they remain steadfast and true to their faith in Him, then only He bestows His Divine Favours on them in the life hereafter, which is permanent and not transitory like this worldly life."

The retort of Ali Zainal Abedeen evoked spontaneous murmurs of admiration from the courtiers who, in spite of themselves, could not help admitting to themselves that he was a true scion of the house of Muhammad (s.a.w.), whose faith in God, whose belief in the cause of Islam, nothing could shake or diminish.

On hearing the murmurs of admiration, Yazid, despite his drunken state, get scared. His reeling head conjured up possiblities of his courtiers staging an uprising against him in favour of Ali Zainal Abedeen. The cunning nature which he had inherited from his crafty father came to his rescue. He feigned a loud laughter and said: "Why are you blaming me, Ali, for what has befallen you all? It was God Who inflicted this punishment on you and your family for your father's obduracy and defiance of my lawful authority. You got what you deserved according to the Will of God."

"No, Oh tyrant," said Ali Zainal Abedeen, "do not dare to distort and misinterpret the words of God. He in His infinite Wisdom gives time and opportunities to men to see whether they act with justice or tyrannically ride rough-shod over the helpless, defenceless people. His punishment always overtakes the tyrants, sooner or later. Does not the Holy Quran narrate the instances of the prophets of God suffering untold hardships at the hands of the people to whom they had come to preach?"

This forthright reply rendered Yazid speechless. His befuddled mind could not think of anything in reply to Ali's retort. One of his subservient courtiers, who was ever anxious to curry favour with him, thought up a plan to relieve the tension that was mounting.

Getting up from his seat, he bowed before the throne and said: "Your Majesty, I beg of you to bestow Husain's favourite daughter Sakina on me as a slave in reward for the services I have rendered to you."

Hardly had the wretch concluded these words when Zainab, who was till then standing silently with her head bowed, with Sakina by her side, got infuriated as she had never been before and in a loud and ringing voice she said: "You wretched, servile minion of Yazid, have you lost all sense of shame that you want to enslave the Prophet's grandchildren? Is there none amongst you to object to the shameless request of this cur?"

Behind Yazid's throne, a velver, gold-embroidered curtain had been drawn where the ladies of his harem were seated. As Zainab was protesting against the preposterous request of the courtier for enslaving Sakina, Yazid's favourite wife, Hinda, entered the enclosure reserved for his harem. She was a devout and pious lady who had, before her marriage with Yazid, served as a lady-in-waiting in Zainab's household during the time of Maula Ali's Khalifate. She had, even after her marriage, retained her love for and devotion to Zainab. Yazid, knowing this, had carefully concealed from her his plans for killing Husain and had taken good care to see that she was not informed about the aftermath of Karbala. When she heard from behind the curtain the voice of Zainab and the mention of enslavement of the grandchildren of the Prophet, she got extremely perturbed. As if by premonition, she had become restless for several days and was seeing in her dreams Zainab and her sister Umme Kulsum, both weeping bitterly and telling her that they had lost their all in this world. She had, as if by intuition, gathered that her evil-minded husband was bent upon some heinous crime which she could not figure out.

When Hnda heard the words of Zainab, she could not contain herself. In a moment of frenzy she rushed out of the enclosure without a veil, demanding to know who had dared to talk about enslaving the children of the Prophet's house. Yazid was so perturbed by his wife, known for her matchless beauty throughout his kingdom, coming into the open court without her veil, contrary to the custom of those days, that he hurriedly shouted orders dismissing the court, gave instructions to Amr Saad to lead the captives to the darkest dungeons in the fort and to await his further orders. He then rushed from his throne and, throwing his robe on Hinda's head, he led her away into his palace. The good lady kept on requesting him to tell her what had transpired that day, who the prisoners were and why somebody had mentioned about the enslavement of the grandchildren of the Prophet. He gave her evasive replies and tried to allay her fears by saying that the prisoners had nothing to do with the Prophet.

The captives' caravan concluded its journey in the dark, desolate dugneon of the fort of Damascus, which was infested with snakes and scorpions. As soon as the doors of the dungeons were locked, both Zainab and Ali Zainal Abedeen engaged themselves in prayers. They both prostrated their heads and prayed to Almighty God to grant them strength and courage to bear what was in store for them. They both thanked Him for sustaining them through their greatest hour of trial, for enabling them to put up with unparalleled humiliations without a word of complaint against His Dispensation,

The Death in Prison

It was dark inside the room of that fort though the sun was blazing in all its glory outside. It would not be correct to call that place a fort because it was in fact a prison; a prison that had been used for years for the confinement of criminals of the worst type. For years it had remained out of use and its stone-walls were damp and crumbling with decay. It was difficult for any person entering the room to see the persons who were kept inside for there was no light but only darkness visible. Only when the eyes could get used to the darkness some figures were discernible in that dark and dreary cell. There were some ladies and children huddled together and there was one man with them lying on a piece of cloth spread on the damp bare floor. If a person were to look closely at the inmates of the cell, he would find that the prisoners wore haggard looks — looks of sorrow, looks of despair and despondency. Those careworn faces were depicting indescribable sufferings. Those emaciated faces were reflecting the calamities suffered beyond human endurance.

Who were the occupants of the cell and what was the crime they had committed which had brought them to such a stage of suffering? If faces could be the index of their character, even a cursory look at them was enough to convince anybody that they were not capable of any offence, much less a heinous crime which alone coud merit the treatment meted out to them. And what possible crime could the ladies and children have committed? Was it the man, young in years but ill and emaciated with privations and sufferings, whose actions had brought so much sufferings to his near and dear ones? Even that did not seem possible because, even in the dark corner of the cell, his head was prostrated in prayers. Could a man, who in the face of such trials and tribulations, did not forget his Maker, who in spite of his illness and sufferings sang the hymns in praise of his Lord, be capable of any atrocious crimes?

Suddenly the door of the cell opened and admitted some light into the cell. In that light it was possible to see that not only the man but even the ladies were engaged in prayers. With the light coming in through that door it was possible to see that all the ladies had grey or white hair. From their faces it was obvious that it was not age that had turned their hair grey but the untold and excruciating pains and pangs of sufferings. Amongst the ladies there was one who was offering her prayers seated. Even a glance at her face was sufficient to reveal the reason why she did so. She looked so emaciated and starved that she did not have the strength to stand up even for a few minutes.

The person who had opened the door brought in a tray on which were placed a few stale morsels of bread. He also had a couple of pitchers of water with him. If you counted the inmates of the cell and the bread that he had brought as their feed, it was obvious that the food could not suffice for all. Could that be the reason for the starvation of the lady? Could it be that she gave her own ration to the children and starved herself? Yes, surely that must be the reason for, how could Zainnb, the sister of Husain, eat her fill when her beloved brother's children, and the children of those who laid down their lives for him, had not enough to eat? Had not Husain, at the time of his last parting, commended the children to her care? Even if he had not done so, Zainab was the daughter of Ali and Fatima, who used to go without food for days together but could not bear to see a prisoner, a wayfarer, or an orphan go hungry.

Somebody has said: "Stone walls do not a prison make; nor iron bars a cage." Perhaps he meant that a prison could confine the bodies of the captives but not their thoughts which soar beyond, breaking all shackles, all barriers. If so, could one imagine where the thoughts of those prisoners were soaring? Yes, it was not difficult to surmise that. The thoughts of each one of them were going back to that plain of Karbala, to the morning when they had with them all those who loved them and whom they loved beyond their lives; to that afternoon when there was an incessant procession of dead bodies being brought in by the aged Imam; to that evening when there was a hush in the battle-field, when there was nothing to be seen near the tents except the dead bodies of those whose strength and valour had only a few hours before struck terror in the hearts of the enemy. And undoubtedly their thoughts were going back to that night when the tents were ablaze, when the thirsty children were running helter-skelter from one burning tent to another, when their belongings were being plundered and looted.

The prisoners partook of their meagre repast and were engaged in prayers again. This was their routine. In some corner some lady who had finished her prayers was trying to suppress the tears that continued to well up in her eyes due to the constant remembrance of the loved ones she had lost on that fateful day. In spite of her best efforts she could not any longer suppress her sobs and weeping. She was weeping to give vent to her pent-up emotions which would otherwise have choked her.

Now the night has descended. But that hardly made any difference, because even during the day it was equally dark inside. For the prisoners there was no more food for the night. The young children drank a little water and went to sleep. As each child drank water, a sob was heard. Was it in remembrance of the brothers, the uncles and father who had died seeking water till the end?

In the dead of night Sakina got up with a shriek. She burst into torrents of tears. Her weeping and wailing aroused everybody. Zainab rushed to her side and tried to console her. "My beloved child," she said, "how often I have told you that the last wish of your father was that you should endure all the sufferings that are inflicted on you with complete resignation to the Will of God?" The child tried to control herself and replied: "Dear Aunt, I know that but, in my dream I saw my father. He came to me and said: 'Oh Sakina you have suffered enough. My darling, the days of your suffering are over. Now I have come to fetch you. Come with me!' O sister of my beloved father, I narrated to him in my dream all the sufferings I had endured since he did not come back from the battle-field. I told him how I had gone in the dark night in search of him. What a dream it was and what a disappointment it is for me to know that in reality I shall be away from my beloved father!" So saying she burst into uncontrollable lamentation. Such was the grief of the child that all the ladies lost control over their emotions and the wail of the ladies echoed through the prison walls.

Yazid in his palace adjoining the prison was pacing the floor. He heard the bemoaning and lamentations and sent for his slaves to enquire about the cause. Soon they hurried back to report what had happened. When Yazid was told that Sakina had seen her father in her dream and was disconsolate, he asked his men to put the head of Husain on a silver salver, cover it with a silken cloth and take it to the prison.

In the dead of night the prison door was opened and Yazid's men entered with the covered tray. They placed it before Sakina. The child cried out: "I am not hungry and I do not want food. I only long to see my father. Why has he left me after promising me that he would not leave me for along?" One of Yazid's attendants removed the cloth from the tray. Sakina beheld the face of her father, the face that she had kissed a million times. It was the same dear, dear face though the beard was smeared with blood. With a cry she flung herself on the tray and snatched the head from it, hugging it to her heart. In indescribable grief she bent down over the head putting her small cheeks against the checks of her father as she used to do when he was alive. Within a few moments her sobs stopped but with it stopped her heart-heats also.

When Zainab saw the child lying motionless on the head of her father, she went over to her and whispered with tears in her eyes: "O Sakina, how long you will lie on your father's head?" She touched her hand only to find that life was extinct, to find that Sakina had gone with her father never to return to this world where she had known nothing but tortures and torments since her becoming an orphan. She realised that her beloved father Husain had kept his promise given to the child in her dream not to leave her in the cell.

Ordeals in Damascus

> *"Eternal spirit of the chainless mind,*
> *Brightest in dungeons liberty thou art"*

Dark though the dungeon always was, it was made more gloomy after Sakina was laid to rest in a grave prepared for her in one corner for her eternal rest, for rest and repose which she had not known since the dawn of the day her father left her, never to return. So long as she was alive, she used to stand near the gratings which were opening on the street to get some fresh air and relief from the suffocating and stifling closeness of the prison atmosphere. Often the passersby used to see her pouring out her grief at the separation from her father. Some kindly ladies even used to halt near the barred opening to ask her who she was and how, in spite of her tender age, she was confined to such a cell. Sakina, on such occasions, used to tell them of her recollections of the byegone days in Medina where, as the daring of her father and her family, her even wish and desire used to be fulfilled, where all the members of her family were vying with one another to keep her happy. She used to recount the events of that fateful day when all her hopes vanished with the last march of her father.

Many of the passersby used to listed to her tale of woes and join her in her tears of agony. Now, whilst passing by the prison, they used to look with anticipation for the innocent face of the child and wonder why she was no more to be seen. Those with more curiosity were even asking the prison-guards as to what had happened to the girl whose face used to be framed in the grating, steeped in sadness and sorrow. The guards were at times telling them to mind their own business and not to let their curiosity land them in trouble. Those guards who had more kindness and feelings in them used to tell such enquirers in hushed tones that the girl they were asking about was sleeping her eternal sleep, freed from the woes and worries of an unkindly world that had denied her every comfort, nay, even consolation, after she had lost her father and her freedom.

Even now at times passersby used to hear prayers offered to God Almighty by the captives at all hours of the day and night. Sometimes the hum of prayers used to be choked by the sobs of some heart-broken mother whose thoughts would go back to the death of her beloved child.

****

A day dawned when there was a stir in the prison. The prison guards were told that, the Queen of Damascus was to visit the prisoners and so everything should be done to make the atmosphere of the cell least obnoxious to Queen Hinda. They were asking one another what possible reason could there be for the Queen to visit the prisoners as she had never done so before.

One of the guards took it upon himself to inform the prisoners about the visit of the Queen and to tell them that, in case she enquired about the treatment received at the hands of the guards, to tell all good things about them and not to utter a word of complaint. When the guard entered the cell, he found that Imam Ali Zainal Abedeen was lying prostrate in prayers. He turned to Fizza, who was the eldest amongst the prisoners, to announce to all the prisoners about the visit of Hinda and to ensure that not a word of complaint was uttered against the treatment meted out to them.

With ushers announcing her arrival, Hinda entered the cell accompanied by a few of her ladies-in-waiting. When her eyes got accustomed to the darkness of the dungeon, she saw some ladies sitting with their heads bowed and faces covered with their tresses. She also saw in one corner the emaciated figure of Ali Zainal Abedeen, with heavy chains and menacles, engaged in prayers. For a few minutes Hinda was perplexed to see a grave in one corner of the cell and one lady resting her head on it. She instinctively went over to that lady and put her hand gently on her head and whispered to her: "My good lady, tell me how you are, to what family you belong and whose grave it is on which you are leaning. I can see from your face that you have suffered untold agonies. For God's sake let me know what is the cause of all your sufferings."

Hinda waited for a while but no reply came to her questions. Instead the lady burst into sobs which made any speech impossible for her. Hinda then turned towards another lady, who sat in a corner, surrounded by several others. She could guess that this lady must be the one whom the others were regarding as the elder and leader amongst them. She recalled from her stature and bearing that this was the lady who, when the prisioners had entered the court of her husband not so long ago, had addressed the court. Though at that time she could not hear what she had said, she could surmise that a person who, even in the helpless state of a prisoner, could muster sufficient courage to hurl defiance at the court, must be possessing unique courage and strength of character. Going over to her she sat down beside her on the bare door, much to the surprise and consternation of her maids and ladies-in-waiting. Addressing her almost reverentially, Hinda said; "I have come to visit you today to learn something from you about the reasons of your sufferings and plight. For a long time I have been trying to find our who you all are, from whar place you come and what heinous crimes you people committed that you are being subjected to this incarceration and made to endure such hardships."

Pausing for a while she continued, "My husband has been evading my enquiries and telling me that I should not concern myself with the affairs of his Government. Of late I have been getting dreams in which I see my lady Fatima, daughter of our beloved Prophet. She comes to me wailing and wringing her hands and telling me, 'Hinda, you are nor aware of what has been done to my son Husain and what has befallen my daughters Zainab and Kulsum and the other ladies and children of our family. You are living in the lap of luxury whilst my children and grand-children are undergoing tortures and torments beyond human endurance'." Speaking softly in a barely audible voice she added: "So often I have seen her in my dreams in a disconsolate state that I find it impossible to rest in peace. Only last night she came to me in my dream and told me that her beloved Husain's daughter, Sakina had been relieved by death from her sufferings and pains. It has dawned on me now that, perhaps, My Lady's coming and bewailing in my dreams had some connection with your incarceration, though I wonder how it could be possible for the family of the Prophet to have anything in common with you all."

The last words of Hinda aroused Zainab from her stupor. She raised her head and looked Hinda full in the face. The eyes of the two ladies met for an instant — the one depicting bewilderment and enquiring, and the other reflecting a soul full of agony and anguish. Zainab's eyes conveyed to Hinda in that one instance volumes of her sufferings which no words, however eloquent, could have conveyed. Zainab could see that Queen Hinda, who not so long ago had been one of her constant companions in the days of her father, could not recognise her. Such was the toll taken by the hardships she had suffered that she could not he recognised even by one who had been so close to her. She reflected that if Hinda did not know who she was, so much the better for her. It would save her the humiliation of narrating all the tortures she had been put to, enumerating the countless indignities site had suffered.

Much though Zainab tried to control her feelings, she could not help hursting into sobs. She had partially covered her face with her hair and she had hoped that Hinda, not recognising her, would leave her without pressing further to know who she was. But Hinda, in that one instant, felt as if she had seen this venerable lady in better times and better circumstances. The lady retaining such dignified mein and bearing and holding her own even in such squalid surroundings, could only be from some family of the highest lineage. Hinda taxed her memory to the inmost extent to recollect when and where she had met her before. She bent over Zainab and parted the hair covering Zainab's face so that she could have a closer look at her. At that very moment she felt she recognised who this lady was. With a gasp she cried: "If my eyes are not deceiving me, I am seeing my Lady Zainab before me! But, my God, how can this be true? Am I imagining the wildest thing possible or seeing a nightmare? O how can it be possible that the daughter of Ali, Leader of the Faithful, and beloved and respected daughter my Lady Fatima, the favourite and beloved sister of Imam Husain, be here in such dismal surroundings, in such abject circumstances? Is my memory playing some cruel trick on me that I see my respected Zainab in the person of this lady on whose face sorrows and sufferings are writ large?"

Hinda, uttering these words, bent further and beseechingly said to Zainab, "O lady, I am at the moment becoming demented by the thought that I see before me the family of the Prophet of Islam, though this very idea is so absurd, so ridiculous and so revolting to me that I consider it almost a blasphemy to entertain it even for a moment. I think I am losing my senses and, unless you tell me who you are, I will get deranged with doubts that are gnawing at my mind. I implore you to let me know, for the sake of my Lady Fatima, who has been coming in my dreams, in what way you are related to my Lady Zainab whom I have been longing to see all these years."

"O lady", with a sob she continued, "if you have any blood relationship with her, tell me when you saw her last and how she was and how were Umme Kulsum, Umme Farwa, Umme Laila and Umme Rabab. I am dying to get news about them and their children who, by God's Grace, must now have grown up, and may even have reached marriageable age."

When Zainab heard these words of Hinda, as if in a flash, she saw before her mind's eyes those young stalwarts, those hopes of the family of Bani Hashim, who were mercilessly slaughtered in Karbala before her eyes. She could see before her mind's eyes the faces of Ali Akbar, Qasim, Aun, Muhammad and the innocent face of Ali Asghar. She could no longer contain herself and she cried, "Hinda, forget Zainab about whom you are talking — that Zainab died on the plains of Karbala with her brother and the youths of the family who were martyred with her brother Husain. Hinda, you see before you the shadow of that Zainab whom neither you, nor any other person can recognise or care to recognise." With these words she hid her face in her hands and wept bitterly.

When Hinda heard this Zainab's anguished outcry, she fell prostrate at her feet. Overcome by contrition, she cried: "Zainab, my lady, forgive me my unpardonable neglect. O God, how could I be so callous as not to understand and recognise that none except my Lady Zainab could have had the boldness to defy my tyrant husband in his court on that day! I implore you, my lady, by the memory of your beloved mother Lady Fatima, to forgive me my sin in not doing anything for your freedom. Oh, how could I live comfortably in my palace, sorrounded by all the pomp and luxuries which money and wordly means can buy, when members of the family of my lord Husain were confined to this dungeon, when his own children were in shackles and hand-cuffs!" Saying this she turned to the corner where Imam Ali Zainal Abedeen was sitting after just completing his prayers. She went over to him and throwing herself at his feet she cried; "Now I can very well recognise you as my Imam Husain's eldest son Ali, who have acquired name and fame throughout, the Islamic realm for piety and prayers."

"O Zainal Abedeen," she sobbed, "I seek your forgiveness for my thoughtlessness in not probing deeper, when my suspicions were aroused on the day of your presentation in my husband's court, when I had distinctly heard some one say that a heartless beast had talked about enslavement and bondage of the Prophet's grand-child." Saying this she looked round her, as if searching for somebody. As she could not find the person whom she was looking for, she continued; "I do not see amongst you the young girl who was with you in court, who was clinging to my Lady Zainab and crying disconsolately. Now I know that she must be the beloved daughter of my lord Imam Husain. Where is she? What has happened to her? Was she at last enslaved by some brute?"

All this while Zainab was sitting with her head bowed. She now stood up and, going towards Hinda, she said, "In vain you are looking for Sakina, my beloved niece, whom my brother had, at the time of his departure, entrusted to my care. She is sleeping peacefully in that yonder grave. She is at last relieved from her pains and sufferings by a kindly death which has given her comforts which, in our state of imprisonment, we could not provide to her."

"May I ask, Zainab, what was the cause of her death?" enquired Hinda. "Did she die because of any disease or because of denial of food and other necessities of life?"

"Hinda," replied Zainab, "how am I to tell you what led to her death. This fragrant flower of our family withered away due to not one but several causes. How can I tell you, Hinda, what sufferings she endured ever since the martyrdom of her father? She was mercilessly slapped, her ear-rings were snatched away most callously and cruelly, tearing her ear-lobes the wounds of which kept on bleeding till the last, because we had been denied all means of treatment. Her young body had become all purple and blue because of injuries sustained by her when repeatedly she used to fall from the bare-back camel she was made to ride during our march from Karabla to your city."

Recounting these sufferings of the child, Zainab was crying, and so was everyone, including Hinda. Only one lady, who was sitting near the grave, was quiet. Her head was resting on the grave and she was lying motionless. Zainab instinctively looked in her direction and seeing that Umme Rabab had swooned and lost her consciousness, she ran towards her and put her head on her lap. Hinda also came over to her and ordered her maids to bring some cold water from the nearby palace. It was brought post-haste according ro Queen Hinda's orders and sprinkled on the face of Umme Rabab. It revived her. Opening her eyes, she looked round her with a dazed look. She faintly utrered, as if in a trance: "My Sakina is sleeping here. Please do not talk loudly as it may disturb her peaceful sleep. She always used to get up from her sleep crying, as she used to dream sometimes of burning of our tents in Karbala, sometimes of the cruel whipping or slapping of her face by Shimr. Now, at long last, she is having an unbroken sleep. Do not, for Allah's sake, wake her up."

Zainab realised that Umme Rabab's grief-striken mind had built up barriers to resist the cruel impact of reality; to create a shelter for her so that she could escape the grief-laden atmosphere around the grave of her child. But she felt that she must be awakened from this stupor now or else she would forever lose her mind. She slowly told her that Sakina had been called away by her father but she should not worry about her. She was now happy and relieved. Her father had responded to her repeated entreaties to come and take her away, to put an end to the pains and pangs, both physical and those of separation. These words brought Umme Rabab back to the world of stark reality. She wept bitterly which lightened the burden on her emotion-packed heart. Hinda and all the ladies who were in the prison, joined her in the mourning.

It is common for people in whose house death occurs to receive people offering sympathies and condolences, to console the grief-stickcn and bereaved members of the family. When Sakina died there were no callers, no mourners, no sympathisers to come and offer comfort to the ladies of the Prophet's house. They were consoling one another. There were no outsiders to take care of the funeral rites of this innocent child. For the first time after so many days Zainab, Umme Kulsum, Umme Rabab and other ladies of their family were having with them sympathetic ladies offering condolences and comforts, sharing their grief, crying with them and uttering words of consolation. What a balm these kind words provided to the grief-torn hearts of Zainab and Umme Rabab can be understood only by those who have been placed in such a predicament. Would to God that nobody may be placed in such a situation in a strange land in a friendless world!

All this while Hinda was thinking furiously about ways and means of securing the freedom of the Prophet's family. She had decided that she would not under any circumstances allow a day to pass without having the prisoners set free and restored to a position of respect and honour which was their right and due. She begged of Imam Ali Zainal Abedeen and Zainab to excuse her for a while and returned to the palace. She called her young son Muawiah, who was the only male issue of Yazid, and told him everything that had transpired that day. Her son had inherited many of her good qualities and he at once told her that he would join her in telling Yazid that, now that they both knew who the prisoners were and what had been done by Yazid to the beloved grandson of the Prophet, they would not live in the palace unless the Prophet's family were restored full liberty and honour.

Hinda and Moawiah both rushed to the private quarters of Yazid where only they had access without any prior announcement. They were surprised to see Yazid pacing up and down and muttering to himself. They could hear him mumble: "Alas, what made me decide to dye my hands with the blood of Husain and the youths of his family! What made me subject the members of his family to indignities and imprisonment! I thought I was removing a thorn from my side but, by doing that, I have lost all peace, all mental equilibrium."

When Yazid saw Hinda coming towards him with her hair dishevelled and her eyes full of tears, followed by his young son Muawiah, whose eyes were also swollen with crying, he was bewildered and surprised. His reverie was broken by their arrival and he wondered what had brought them to him in such a condition. However, before he could ask them the reasons and the purpose of their visit, Hinda narrated to him her dreams leading up to her visit to the prison and what she had seen and heard that day. She was beside herself with grief and rage and, ignoring the consequences of her tyrant husband's wrath, she plainly told him that she and her son had decided that, if members of the Prophet's family were not set free that very day, both of them would denounce him for the tyrant that he was, no matter whether he beheaded them or threw them into the dungeons or subjected them to the worst kind of tortures.

Yazid was not accustomed to this kind of talk from his Queen who, much as she detested and dispised his despotic ways, was always gentle and soft-spoken. He was stupefied and for sometime rendered speechless by the bold and dauntless attitude of his wife and son.

Thinking that Yazid was considering some diabolical plans to punish them for the defiance they had hurled at him, Muawiah said, "Father, young though I am, I realise that what my mother says is the only honourable course we can now adopt. All these days we remained ignorant of what had happened because of our callousness. May God forgive us for our neglect and our failure to alleviate the sufferings of my lord Imam Husain's family. The situation does not admit of a moment's delay and we want you to decide here and now what you intend to do in this matter."

Cunning and crafty as Yazid was, he knew that his cup of cruelty was getting filled to the brim. His sccrel agents had reported to him that, after Sakina's death, many ladies of Damascus were taunting their husbands, brothers and sons and accusing them of cowardice in not doing anything for the liberation of the family of the Prophet. Many men were talking secretly about ways and means of securing freedom for the ladies of the house of Imam Husain, and Imam Ali Zainal Abedeen. They were asking one another what the prisoners had done to deserve such prolonged imprisonment in a dungeon. He could now see the writing on the wall. Realisation now dawned on him that time was running out for him, that nemesis might over-take him unless he did something to save the situation. Now that his own son, his own flesh and blood, and his Queen Hinda, were also asking for, nay even demanding, the liberation of the prisoners, he could see which way the wind was blowing. In his crooked mind a thought came that if he agreed to set free the prisoners now, he might be able to save his face and say to outsiders that he did it in deference to the wishes of his own wife and son and not by way of succumbing to popular demand. His warped mind was always apprehending that, if he bowed to the wishes of his subjects, then he may lose his authority over them. In his heart of hearts he had a fear that the public may accept Imam Ali Zainal Abedeen as their leader and dethrone him. At the same time, coupled with concern for the safety of his throne, he had within him a deep-rooted feeling of remorse which was exacerbated by the nightmares he was getting. For days together he had not been getting any sleep. Whenever he would close his eyes, he would see the Prophet standing before him, full of grief, upbraiding him and asking him: "O Yazid, what had my Husain done to deserve your vengence? What made you destory my family with such vengefulness and brutality? Is your hatred for me and my family still not satiated that you are subjecting the widows and orphans of my family to such inhuman tortures?" He was constantly haunted by such dreams and he had been brooding about the ways and means of resolving the dilemma that was confronting him and which was very much of his own creation. That instant he decided that the time was most opportune for him to set free the prisioners and to send them away from Damascus as early as possible so that his position and power may not be endangered, his authority may not be dented.

"What a strange way of pleading for mercy and clemency you have adopted," said Yazid, turning towards his wife. "If both of you are so much filled with pity and sympathy for the prisoners, could you not plead for them in a better way than remonstrating before me in this fashion?" He paused for a while to see the reaction of his words on them and then continued, "I am glad to accede to the request of both of you and to set free the prisioners honourably. I am summoning my court and announcing my decision immediately. Now both of you may rest in peace and let me also have some respite after the shock you have administered to me by your remonstralions."

"Peace, did you say?" said Hinda in surprise. "Can you think that I, or my son, can ever have peace in this life after knowing what you did to the grandson of Prophet Muhammad, and his family, in furtherance of your diabolical designs? Are the things you did, even after the massacre of Karbala, not enough to make us hang our heads in shame and fill our hearts with remorse and contrition? Would to God that I had nor lived to see this day, to know that my lord Imam Husain's beloved daughter Sakina was dying by inches in the dungeon, while I was living in comfort, oblivious of her sufferings, ignorant of the ordeals and handships of my ladies Zainab, Rabab and others of the Prophet's family and Imam Ali Zainal Abedeen!" Saying this she wept bitterly.

After a while she continued, "Yazid, I want you, for the sake of Allah and His Prophet, if you at all have any belief in them, to make best amends for the unforgivable atrocities you have perpetrated, for the unpardonable silts you have committed. Spare no efforts in repairing the damage and loss you have caused to the people of the

Prophet's house, for whom God has carved out a niche of honour and respect in the hearts of all true believers. It may perhaps be too late to redeem your sinning soul from the eternal perdition which you have earned for yourself by your atrocious actions, still the least that you can do now is to restore Imam Ali Zainal Abedeen, and the venerable ladies who are with him, to the place of honour which is their right."

Muawiah, who was standing quietly by his mother's side all this while, shedding tears silently, joined his mother in asking for full restitution for the family of the Imam. With full assurance from Yazid that he would leave no stone unturned in doing so, they left him.

Yazid lost no time in summoning his court that very same day. He issued orders to his Court Minister to place a pulpit next to his throne and to make special arrangements, with curtains and draperies drawn for the ladies of the family of Imam Husain. Instructions were despatched post-haste to call an iron-smith for cutting and removing the shackles, manacles and chains in which Imam Ali Zainal Abedeen, and others with him, were bound.

It was late in the evening when the court was assembled. There was full display of all the regalia associated with the Ummayad court. Yazid was seated on the throne, decked in a jewelled dress of silk and brocade All the dignitaries of the realm were present, dressed in their best garments. All the accredited representatives of friendly foreign countries were seated in their chairs to witness an event of which they had no prior intimation. Many were puzzled at the manner in which the court had been summoned at such a short notice, contrary to the custom and practice of Yazid's Government, They were asking each other what could be the occasion for the holding of the court. Some were even hazarding guesses which were nothing but flights of fancy.

Those present in the court had not long to wait as the ushers announced, with all solemnity, that the great-grandson of Prophet Muhammad, Imam Ali Zainal Abedeen was entering the court and the venerable ladies of his household were gracing the occasion by their presence behind the curtains which had been drawn for them. They saw Imam Ali Zainal Abedeen enter the court and walk over to the pulpit with a slow, halting gait, as if despite removal of the chains, his aching, lacerated legs were finding the walk an ordeal. Most of them, who were present in this same court when Imam Ali Zainal Abedeen, and the ladies of his family were some months before brought in chains in the court, were shocked to see that time and tortures had taken a very heavy toll and the Imam was emaciated and attenuated to such an extent that, but for the ushers' announcement, it would have been difficult for them to recognise him. His garments were also torn and tattered. But, in spite of all this, there was dignity in his bearing, there was a radiance on his countenance, a halo on his face, which inspired awe in their hearts. As if drawn by the magnetism of his personality, they all stood up from their seats to do homage to the personality of this noble scion of the Prophet's house who had borne tortures and torments, who had suffered insults and indignities but never for a moment wavered, never for an instant, faltered in his resolve, never for a second thought of asking for any favours or any facility for himself, or even for the ladies and children who were suffering with him. Seeing this spontaneous gesture of the courtcors, Yazid also got up from his throne, as if impelled by an uncontrollable force. The Imam slowly mounted the pulpit saying "In the name of Allah, the Most Beneficent, the Most Merciful." There was pin-diop silence in the court which was only broken by the rustling of the curtains indicating that, simultaneously with Imam Ali Zainal Abedeen, Zainab and the other ladies with her, had entered the court through the separate entrance reserved for them and had taken their seats in the curtained enclosure behind the pulpit.

After Imam Ali Zainal Abedeen had taken his seat on the pulpit, Yazid broke the silence by offering him condolences on the passing away of young Sakina. His words of sympathy were sounding so hollow in the light of his callous conduct throughout that he hurriedly changed the subject and started offering his apologies for all that had happened. As if to save his face, he started cursing Obeidullah Ibne Zaid, Amr Ibne Saad and Shimr Ziljaashan for giving him wrong information about the aims of Imam Husain. Prerending utmost contrition, he expressed profound regrets at all that had transpired in Karbala and the subsequent events upto that day. In an abject tone, he told the Imam that he and his family were now free to stay where they liked, to go where they liked. He also offered to the Imam whatever amount he named as "blood money" for the martyrs of his family. When he mentioned this, the Imam's face turned red with rage. Seeing this, Yazid hurriedly added; "O Ali Zainal Abedeen, what I am offering is permitted by our religious code and I beseech you to accept it."

Before Imam Ali Zainal Abedeen could reply to him, Zainab, who was listening to the talk from behind the curtain, cried out, "O Yazid, are you nor satisfied with wounding our feelings and torturing us all these days that you want to re-open our hearts' wounds by this offer? If you think that your wealth can undo what you have done to the family of the Prophet, you offer what you possess on the day of reckoning to the Prophet himself when he questions you about his grandson."

She wept copiously and then continued: "O Yazid, it is not for us to accept any requital, recompense or blood money for those who were martyred by your orders. If you have called us today with the expectation that we will accept what you want to offer to us, you are very much mistaken. Your actions will be judged by Allah and His Prophet and you will have to answer to them for your tyrannies on the Day of Judgement."

Yazid was abashed by the bold retort of Zainab. He had experience of her courage and defiance when she had first time appeared in his court in the most trying circumstances. He knew that, if he dared to say anything more, he would get from her even stronger rebuff. He immediately changed the subject and, addressing Imam All Zainal Abedeen, he said, "O Grandson of the Prophet, you are free now to demand anything that I have. I am issuing orders that a house be placed at your disposal and you may be accorded the treatment befitting your dignity and status in life. It is now for you to decide whether you desire to stay on in Damascus or leave for Madina. Your respected aunt Zainab and your family have my solemn assurances that henceforth highest honour and respect will be extended to you all as befits those belonging to the family of the Prophet of Islam."

Imam Ali Zainal Abedeen informed Yazid that he did not want anything from his wordly possessions. He added that all that he wanted was the servered heads of the martyrs of Karbala which had been kept in his vaults, and their looted property and clothes of which they had been robbed and deprived on the evening of the tragedy of Karbala.

This reply evoked considerable surprise in Yazid. He could not understand how a person could turn his face away from the offer of all the good things of life which he had made. Suppressing his surprise Yazid remarked: "O Zainal Abedeen, I have seen all the belongings of you and your family which were looted by my army in Karbala. I could not see in them anything of value. Except for the house-hold articles and clothes, which were all well-worn, there were no ornaments, jewels or articles of gold and precious stones."

When Zainab heard these words of Yazid, she could not contain herself. Before Imam Ali Zainal Abedeen could say anything in reply, she spoke up, "How can we explain to you, Yazid, how we value our belongings which have incalculable sentimental value for us? Amongst the articles, which were snatched away at the time of our capture in Karbala, are the veil which my mother Fatima Zahra used to wear and which I inherted from her on her death. There is also the blood-stained garment worn by my brother Husain when he was beheaded by Shimr. It was woven by my mother with her own hands. There are garments soaked in the blood of our sons, nephews and other kith and kin. There are ear-rings which were snatched away from the ears of my dearest Sakina, tearing her ear lobes. Can anything you possess or all that your wealth can purchase, match these raiments and articles? No, Yazid, we shall cherish these things as our most precious possession till the end of our days."

Realising that utmost sentimental value was placed on the looted articles by Zainab and the other members of Imam Husain's family, Yazid ordered his men to restore all these objects to them immediately. He also issued orders that a house may be placed at their disposal and all kinds of facilities and amenities may be provided to them. On his enquiries, Imam Ali Zainal Abedeen informed him that, he and the members of his family, did not want to slay long in Damascus but wanted to return to Madina; but before they did so, they wanted to visit Karbala to bury the martyrs' heads which were now given over to them.

After this brief session the court was adjourned and the Imam and his family were taken to the house near the palace which was placed at their disposal. Queen Hinda insisted on accompanying Zainab and Umme Kulsum as a lady-in-waiting, performing the duties which she was performing in the days of yore at Kufa.

On reaching the house, Zainab found that a large number of ladies and men had collected there. On her enquiring about the purpose of their visit, she was told that the populace of Damascus had come on a condolence visit. The men surrounded Imam Ali Zainal Abedeen and offered condolences to him. The ladies of Damascus went over to the separate quarters where ladies of the Prophet's family were sitting and, going over to each one of them, offered their sympathies. Many amongst them were asking for details of the tragedy. Some were asking them about Sakina, whose days in Damascus as a prisioner were so fresh in their minds and whose ordeals, from the day she had entered the city's portals, were vividly remembered by them. Zainab, on behalf of all the ladies, recounted to them all the events, from the day they left Medina to the fateful day when they lost all whom they loved in the world, who were dearer to them than their lives. She narrated each incident with tears flowing torrentially from her eyes. All the other ladies of the family, and the ladies of Damascus were shedding tears with her. She even recalled in details the days passed in Damascus, from the day of their entering the city to the day when Sakina, unable to bear the miseries and torments indicted on her, had surrendered her young and innocent life to her Maker. She also described the events leading upto their release and mentioned her desire to go back to Karbala to bid a final farewell to all the dear departed ones whose bodies they had left on the burning sands of Karbala without any cover, without even shrouds.

With one voice all the ladies persuaded Zainab and other members of her family to stay on in Damascus. Their menfolk also used their best persuasions to make Imam Ali Zainal Abedeen stay on in Syria. But nothing they said could change the decision of the Imam and his family to leave Damascus.

Under orders of Yazid, canopied camels and best horses were procured for the journey to Karbala. All the citizens of Damascus had turned out to bid farewell to the Prophet's family. Men, women and children were crying as one by one the ladies, assisted by the Imam, ascended their mount. Hinda, who had all along remained with Zainab to offer solace and comfort to her in the best manner possible, went from one lady to another offering her sympathies and asking for forgiveness for the previous neglect on her part. She was about to leave when she heard Umme Rabab express her wish to Zainab that, before leaving Damascus, they may visit the prison and offer their last Fateha at the grave of young Sakina. Zainab immediately assented to this suggestion and, with Hinda accompanying them, the caravan wended its way towards the prison-house. The Imam and all the ladies dismounted and went over to the grave of Sakina. The disconsolate mother fell on the grave with a heart-rending shriek. "Sakina, my darling," she cried, "we all are free at last, but it is your lot to remain forever and forever within the four walls of this prison. My dearest child, I am leaving you alone in this strange country, where you had experienced nothing but hardships, torments and tortures. My child, I am leaving you but my heart and soul will remain with you in this prison." Saying this, she turned to Hinda and the other ladies of the town who had joined them and whispered, "I am leaving my dearest daughter in your midst. There is none from our family in this city to visit her grave, to offer Fateha and flowers. I beseech you, once in a way to visit my lonely, luckless child's grave for offering Fateha and flowers." With these words she fell unconscious in the arms of Zainab.

The Journey's End

"Princess, if our aged eyes,
"'Weep upon thy matchless wrongs;
It's because resentment ties,
The terrors of our tongues".

It was evening of 30th Muharram 61 in Medina, the city of the Prophet, on which a kind of gloom had descended since that day in the holy month of Rajab when Imam Husain and his family left it on their fateful journey. The lowering clouds were darker than usual as if they were gathering on the evening blast to herald some happening of very great and grave import. Many elderly people in the bazaars were exchanging meaningful glances with each other as if they were having premonition of some momentous events or some upheaval of far-reaching effect. Some of them, feeling intuitively a heaviness of heart, were rushing towards the tomb of the Prophet to seek solace and comfort there, as was their wont on such occasions. A few more superstitious amongst them were feeling apprehensive as if some doom were to descend on them. The atmosphere had become so close and suffocating that men, women and children rushed out of their houses to breathe the air outside. Accustomed as the inhabitants of Medina were to the oppressive heat at times experienced in that oasis, they could not help remarking that on this particular evening, it was not only heat that was stifling them but something besides, inscrutable, inexplicable, unescapable and ominous, presaging and foreboding something calamitous.

Those of the inhabitants of Medina who had gone out of

the town to rest in the palm-groves in the suburbs saw a cloud of dust rising in the distant horizon. When the dust had settled down, they saw a few riders galloping post-haste towards the city. The youngmen, anxious to know who the riders were and why they were riding at such break-neck speed, mounted their colts and went out to meet them. When they came near the riders, they enquired who they were and why they were riding their steeds so fast. The riders did not stop their chargers to reply to the enquiries but rode on, gesturing to them to follow them to the city, if they fell interested to know what they had come to herald in Medina. Following this hint, those youngmen harkened all their friends and compasnions to return to the town to hear the proclamation which the despatch-ridcrs were obviously carrying from the rulers in Damascus.

As the King's couriers entered the limits of Medina, more and more people joined them. They all followed the dispatch riders to the tomb of the Prophet. The town-crier was summoned by the Governor of Medina, who had also repaired to the Prophet's mosque on learning about the arrival of the King's heralds. He ordered a drum to be beaten, summoning all able-bodied citizens to gather at the tomb of the Prophet for hearing the important announcement and the proclamation. Very soon a huge throng was collected and the Mosque adjoining the tomb was packed to capacity. In their anxiety to hear the momentous news, people forgot the oppressive heat and choking closeness of the atmosphere. Deep down within them every man, woman and child had a feeling, rather a foreboding that something calamitous was in store for them; some tidings of disaster were coming to them.

When the mosque was jampacked with men, women and children, in a loud and stentorian voice the herald from Damascus proclaimed: "O people of Medina, be it known to you all that Husain, son of Ali, and grandson of the Prophet, who had left Medina with his kith and kin and followers and who had refused to owe allegiance to the Leader of the Faithful, Yazid, son of Moawiah, was engaged in a battle on the plains of Karabala and he and his followers and supporters were put to the sword. His womenfolk were taken prisoners along with the children. They were taken to Damascus, with the severed heads of Husain and his followers, and paraded through the streets of Kufa and Damascus so that their plight may serve as an object lesson to those who may dare ro defy the authority of the Ruler." The court messenger paused for a while to see the effect produced by his announcement. The pin-drop silence was broken by the heaving of sighs which escaped the lips of all those assembled there as if in unision. Many burse into sobs. Several ladies and children shrieked and swooned. An angry outburst of remonstration escaped the lips of quite a few valiant ones. Sensing that it was necessary to nip all trouble in the bud, the messenger shouted at the top of his voice his command to silence the gathering. Once again pin-drop silence descended on the gathering and the hearald continued: "I am ordered by Yazid bin Moawiah to proclaim to you that he has sepatately conveyed ro the Governor of Medina instructions to exterminate those of you who in any way, by words or deeds, show any feelings or sympathy for Husain bin Ali, grandson of the Prophet, or the members of his faimly or his followers, whatever your relationship or family ties with them may be. Any disregard of this warning would not only invite direst consequences and calamity on the person showing such recalcitrance but also on his entire family. The punishment for any expression of support, or even sympathy, for the people of the Prophet's house will not stop at the death of the person concerned but would lead to the extirpation of his entire family."

The ominous words of the king's emissary rendered the audience dumbfounded. They were all hushed into an errie silence as if some magic spell had been cast round them. The silence was only intermittently broken by sonic uncontrollable sobs or stifled cries of agony, involuntarily escaping the lips of some grief-striken ladies. The Governor of Medina and the messengers from Damascus, including the person who had read out the proclamation, sat silently surveying the situation. They appeared to be pleased with the effect their threat had produced on the assemblage and they were waiting as if to let the effect further sink into the hearts of the terror-srriken people.

Suddenly they saw an aged lady, draped in veil, tearing through the gathering and advancing towards the dais where the Governor and the messengers from Damascus were seated. She was holding the hand of a lad who appeared to be hardly five or six years old. She was walking with such dignified gait that all the faces were turned towards her in awe.

The lad, whose hand was held tightly by the venerable lady, was making efforts to free himself from her grip. Young though he was, he seemed to be possessing extra-ordinary strength as, with a little effort, he was able to extricate himself from the firm hold of the lady and run like a gazel through the hushed multitude towards the podium where the Governor and the emissaries from Damascus were seated, studying the reaction which their pronouncement had produced on the gathering with a feeling of relief and triumph. Their gaze now turned in the direction of the boy who was now heading towards them. He jumped on the platform and with a look of expectancy and innocence he asked the person who had just read the proclamation: "Has my father arrived? Where is he now?" These abrupt questions, which were shot at the announcer in rapid succession, made him pucker his brows in wonder at the boldness of the child. In particular he was amazed at the tone in which the questions were put, a tone of self assurance and authority seldom to be heard from a child of such tender age. As if he had heard a command which called for an immediate response, he replied; "My lad, before I reply to your questions, just let me know who you are and who is your father, about whom you are enquiring."

As if the boy considered this enquiry a display of ignorance or impertinence, he raised his chin further and retorted: "Don't a you know my father? Are you not an Arab that you show ignorance about me and my family." Saying this he, with characteristic innocence turned his face to the vast multitude of Medinites thronged there and gesturing with his small hands and pointing in their direction, he continued: "Ask any one of them, O stranger to this city, and they will tell you I am Fuzail, son of Abbas, Standard-bearer of my Lord Imam Husain's army and his most beloved brother." With those words he turned towards the Governor of Medina who was observing with dumbfounded amazement the boldness of the child so characteristic of the family of Ali and his children. Nonchalantly addressing the Governor he said, "Why don't you tell this man who I am and who my father is? By God, why is he delaying in replying to my question?"

By this lime the old lady accompanying this child had reached the dais. When he had lessened her hold on his hand and run towards the platform, she had quickened her pace apprehending that if the people who had assembled in the mosque rose to disperse, there might be a stampede with considerable danger of her charge being trampled under foot. When she saw the child reach the dais without any misphap, she was greatly relieved. Still she continued her advance at a brisk pace, apprehending that the child might be subjected to some kind of tortures by the sadistic Governor. On her way to the Mosque, she had heard the announcement about the martyrdom of Imam Husain. On reaching the dais she mounted it and took hold of the child's hand. Turning to the emissary from Damascus she said, "O harbinger of bad tidings, tell me when Husain and his sons and followers were butchered by the tyrant of Damascus and his henchmen, where was my son Abbas? Did he not shed the last drop of his blood in defending the Imam and his family? Where were my other sons Muhammad and Usman and Jafar? How could Husain and his sons be butchered mercilessly with my four sons there to defend them?" These words were spoken by the lady in a loud, clear, ringing voice which could be heard far and wide in the stillness that had descended on that gathering. Her words had an electrifying effect on the congregation and an involuntary and spontaneous sigh of admiration escaped the lips of thousands.

The herald from Damascus regained his composure in

the fraction of a minute and turning to the lady replied: "Did you not hear me proclaim that all the kith and kin of Husain, his borthers, his sons, his nephews and his followers, were all put to the sword? What makes you, think that your sons were not amongst them? For your edification let me add that your sons, in particular Abbas, put up a fight the like of which has not been seen in this part of the world and which will be talked about for a long time to come, wherever and whenever deeds of bravery are admired and discussed by men."

Fatema Qalabiya or Ummul Baneen, as she was popularly known, heard these words in silence. For a moment she stared with glassy eyes as if she were dumbstruck. Her face became ashen pale. Her lips, which were parched dry, were moving as if to say something but no words escaped from them. She was staring hard as if she was seeing some scene in her mind's eye, a kaleidoscope, the meaning of which she could not piece together. She neither swooned nor uttered a cry. Her grandson Fuzail who was beside her, was looking up intently at her as if he too were struck by the evil tidings. He instinctively felt that his grandmother, in spite of her desperate attempt to control her surging feelings, was overcome by grief. Clutching her hands, he cried; "Grandmother, what has come over you? Why don't you say something? Why do you not tell this man that what he says cannot be true — that no man is born who can kill my father and uncles, the most brave, the most gallant, the most valiant of mankind?"

Ummul Baneen's reverie was broken by the child's urgent though innocent pleadings. She looked round to see that all eyes were rivetted on her and her grandson beside her. In a moment she decided that she should not do anything which might invoke the pity of the assemblage. She felt that she owed it to the memory of her brave sons not to say or do anthing which might be construed as weakness of the mother of one so fearless, hold and gallant as Abbas. She would rather fight a battle with the great feelings of anguish which were raging within her, feelings of sorrow and indescribable grief which only a mother can feel on hearing the news of death of her sons in the prime of their youth — not one son but four sons whom she had brought up with loving and tender care as the only hope and solace of her bleak life, the life of a widow.

Tightening her grip on the hand of Fuzail she turned away and slowly descended the dais. Her steps, which were firm and fast when she had ascended the platform a little while before, were now slow and heavy. She was walking as if every step required effort on her part. Her head was bowed and her gait was slow. Instead of holding the hand of the child in her firm grip, she had now kept it on his shoulder as if she needed to do so for support. All the eyes in the congregation were following the venerable lady as she and her grandson were trudging out of the Prophet's mosque. Many of them were wondering whither she was bound. Some of them, solicitous about her condition, even followed her, walking a respectable distance behind her. The assembly was now dispersing. Quite a few were rushing home to convey the evil tidings they had received to other members of their family and those of their friends and acquaintances who could not come to the Probhct's mosque.

Ummul Banecn, with Fuzail to support her, slowly made her way to Jannat-ul-Baqi, the graveyard where Fatima, the Prophet's daughter lay buried. As soon as she reached the grave of Husain's mother, Ummul Baneen flung herself on it and, no longer able to control the feelings, which were surging in her heart she burst out; "My lady, I have come to offer my condolences on the martyrdom of your beloved son Husain. I do not mourn my sons Abbas, Muhammad, Usman and Jafar, because I had reared them from their childhood to regard Husain as their lord and master and to live for him and to die for him." With these words she cried her heart out to unburden her soul which was choked with grief. When she slightly regained her composure she continued; "O my lady, my only consolation is that my beloved Abbas, and my other sons fought bravely to the last in defence of Husain. You from heaven must have seen them each dying valiantly as great sons of a great father." Fuzail, who stood crying beside her, tugged at her sleeves to say that quite a number of people were now gathered round them. She looked up to see through her tear-filled eyes that most of the people were weeping for her, sharing the sorrows of a mother whose all hopes for the future were shattered that day by the sad tidings of not one but four martyrdoms of her sons.

With a jerk Ummul Baneen straightened up as if somebody had reminded her of some duty which she had to perform. She remembered that Fatima Sughra, the beloved daughter of Imam Husain whom he had left behind in Medina was lying on her sick-bed. She felt remorse at not going over to her and consoling her. A thought crossed her mind that if some others reached her before her and conveyed the sad news of the carnage of Karbala and told her that her father, her brothers, uncles and cousins had all been put to the sword, she would succumb to the shock of it. She realised that her first and foremost duty was to rush to her bed-side and to gently break the news to her in the best manner she could, after explaining the events to the venerable Umme Salma, wife of the Prophet, who was looking after Fatema Sughra and tending to her in her illness. The high sense of duty, which her son Abbas had acquired from her in such large measure, put a new spirit in her grief-striken frame, from which the sad tidings of that day had only a little while ago sapped all the strength. She once again took hold of the child's hand and, after casting a look around her, as if to convey to the people who were assembled there that, deep as her sorrow was, she was not oblivious of the call of her duty, she walked away briskly. Fuzail was greatly surprised to see that his grandmother, who only a few minutes before had become so benumbed with sorrow that she could hardly walk with heavy steps and needed to support herself by leaning on his young shoulders, was now rushing along, almost running, and dragging him in the process, as if some one had bekoned to her. He knew that any thought of a duty to be performed always electrified the step of that venerable old lady. In his childish imagination he wondered whether his father or his uncle, who he now knew were in heaven, had harkened to her towards some task which needed her attention. He looked up at her with enquiring eyes, to find out why she was walking so briskly, so fast, but his question froze on his lips. He saw his grandmother staring steadfastly with glassy eyes from which tears were rolling down her wrinkled checks. For the first time he saw wrinkles on that face; for the first time he saw her hair gone grey.

When Ummul Baneen took the turning at the cross-roads, Fuzail knew where she was hastening. Young though he was, he knew that she was rushing towards the house of

Imam Husain, where the Prophet's widow Umme Salma was staying with the ailing daughter of the Imam. When both of them reached the house, Ummul Baneen looked round to see that some ladies were standing it a little distance from the house,, discussing something. It did not require much imagination for her to surmise that they were discussing how best to break the news to Fatema Sughra and Umme Salma. She was very much relieved to see that she was not too late in performing this delicate but painful duty of gently informing them about the news of the disaster that had befallen the family of the Prophet.

When the ladies of Medina saw Ummul Baneen, they hastened towards her and one of them conveyed to her what she had already imagined about the problem which was baffling them. She very gently thanked all the ladies for their solicitude and requested them not to visit Fatema Sughra's house as she apprehended that the sight of all of them visiting the house together might administer a shock to her, which she, in her failing health, might not be able to hear. Many of the ladies with sympathy and tears offered her condolences on the death of her four sons, all in the prime of youth, whom she had lost in one day. This reminder of her colossal loss opened up the ghastly wounds in her heart which she had tried to repair with almost super-human control. The mention of her sons' names recalled to her the scene before this very house, in this very street, when one after the other they had come to hid her goodbye. She remembered how affectionately each of them had hugged her in the parting embrace and asked her to look after herself and to remember them in her daily prayers. She recalled how every day, on waking up from her sleep, she would wonder where they were and when they would return to bring back light and life into her drab and dreary world. But now, alas, those fond hopes were all dashed to the ground. For her there was nothing left but to pass her dismal days with the memories of her sons, from the days each one of them sat on her lap and asked her to recount the deeds of bravery of their valiant father, the prowess and feats of arms of their sire which had become almost legendary, how she had recounted to them, times out of number, about the devotion and attachment of their father to the holy Prophet and how she had been exhorting them to imbibe the same spirit and emulate his example, not only in the feats of arms but in his sense of duty and devotion by sparing nothing in the course of their duty towards their elder brothers Hasan and Husain whom she regarded with utmost reverence and loved with deepest affection.

All this passed before the mind's eye of Ummul Baneen in a matter of seconds. As soon as the thought crossed her mind that all that she had inculcated in her sons had not gone in vain and they had lived and died, true to her teachings, she felt a relief as if some soothing balm had been applied to her bleeding heart. She regained her composure and brushed aside her tears. She profoundly thanked all the ladies who had offered her sympathies and requested them to visit the house of Imam Husain after some time to offer condolences to Umme Salma and Fatenia Sughra after she had gently conveyed the sad tidings to them.

When Ummul Baneen entered the room of Fatima Sughra, she saw her restlessly tossing on her couch with Umme Salma, the venerable old widow of the Prophet, sitting with her hand on Sughra's forehead. Seeing her entering the room, Fatima Sughra sat up in her bed, partly out of respect for her grandmother, partly in anticipation of receiving some news from her. A look at the face of Ummul Baneen conveyed volumes to her. The rays of the setting sun were lighting up the tear-stained wrinkled face of Ummul Baneen and the grey hair that she had got that day. Fatema Sughra had been seeing her grandmother daily, the very picture of robust health and vitality. The sight of her, standing before her, aged and bent with the crushing blow that the news had dealt to her, made Sughra feel that her worst fears had come true. Not long ago, she had one night dreamt in the month of Muharram, precisely on the tenth night of that month, that the Prophet had come to her house and put his hand on her head soothingly, much as was customary to do for orphans. She had seen the Prophet in her dream with his clothes soiled with dust and his beard smeared with blood. She had got up from her nightmare with a shriek. At that very moment she had seen her great-grand mother, Umme Salma, getting up from her dream with shrieks. She too had dreamt seeing the Prophet in a similar condition, telling her that he had just returned from the plain of Karbala after seeing his beloved grandson Husain being massacred with his sons, brothers, nephews and faithful friends. Both of them had become painfully conscious of some terrible news reaching them.

Fatema Sughra's health had, since that night, taken a turn for the worse and she had almost become bed-ridden now. A second look at her grandmother's face convinced her that her worst forebodings had come true, that she was seeing in reality what the dream had prepared her for. Umme Salma, with the wisdom of her years, could very well imagine what news Ummul Baneen had come to break to them. There is no way that can be termed gentle in breaking news of such a stupendous disaster. She only exchanged one meaningful glance with Ummul Baneen and understood what had happened. But Fatema Sughra with great efforts cried out in agony of her soul: "Grandmother, for the sake of God tell me the truth. Is my father killed? Are my dear brothers Ali Akbar and Ali Asghar, my loving uncles, all killed? Is it true that I shall never be able to see them in this world?" Saying this she, for a moment, beseechingly looked into the eyes of Ummul Baneen. She tried to say something but no words escaped her parched lips; they only quivered speechlessly. But the big warm tears rolling down her cheeks, which were glistering in the rays of the setting sun, and the nod of her head, conveyed the reply to Fatima Sughra. The grief was too great for her frail body and afflicted mind to bear. With one gasp she fell unconscious on the bed. Umme Salma and Ummul Baneen for the moment forgot their own grief and turned towards Fatema Sughra lest she may also leave them to join her father and brothers and uncles in heaven. Now both these venerable ladies were concerned about this charge left with them and their thoughts turned towards the ladies of Imam Husain's house who had accompanied him to Karbala. They both wondered where they were, what had befallen them, and when they would return to tell them about the events of that bleak day that had seen such gory events.

****

The moon was almost selling, casting its dying rays on the waters of rivulet Al Quma and the few tents that were pitched on its banks. Besides these tents, there were a few graves which were scattered over some distance, providing the only landscape which the lunar beams could light up dimly. The stillness of the night was almost suffocating. The only noise that could be heard for minutes around was the chirping of the night insects and the monotonous rippling of the waters of the Stream. In the eerie atmosphere that was pervading the plain one could almost imagine that the waters of the rivulet were singing a dirge, recounting the mournful events of the day that had seen the death of those who lay buried in the nearby graves.

Suddenly there was a stir in one of the tents, as if somebody had been awakened from his sleep. The flap of the tent was lifted and an old man, walking with a bent back and supporting himself on a staff, came out of it followed by a young person who apparently was his valet or orderly. Slowly he advanced towards the other tents and, standing a few paces away, shouted for the inmates of the other tents to come out. Apparently the old man was speaking with a tone of authority as, hearing his voice, the other persons sleeping in the tents rushed out showing apparent concern for his safety and welfare. He seemed to be their leader or chieftain as they reverentially addressed him with bent heads. One of these persons, who perhaps was closer to him, a friend if not a blood relation, and quite advanced in age, came hurriedly to where the old man was standing and said, "O Jabir, what is the matter with you that you woke up so early before the break of dawn. May Allah bless you and your noble revered father, we all felt frightened by the thought that some illness had come to you or some pain had awakened you from your sleep. Pray tell us the cause of your perturbation, if it is not connected in any way with your health."

The old man was no other than Jabir bin Abdullah Ansari.

He had, on hearing about the martyrdom of Imam Husain and his compansions and the imprisonment and incarceration of the surviving members of his family, had hastened towards Karbala with his devoted friends and followers. He had heard that the bodies of the martyrs of Karbala were left without any burial. He recalled on hearing this that long ago the Prophet of Islam had told him that, after the martyrdom of his beloved grandson Husain, he would participate in the duty of burying the heads of the martyrs on the banks of Al Quma, a tributary of the Euphrates. On reaching Karbala he saw that the Bani Asad, who were having their nomadic camps some distance away from Karbala, had covered the bodies with sand to protect them from the ravages but no proper burial had been given to the martyrs. Jabir Ibne Abdullah Ansari, with the help of his friends prepared the graves of the martyrs. He buried Imam Husain and next to his grave he put the bodies of his two beloved sons, Ali Akbar and Ali Asghar. He put the body of Habib Ibne Mazahir in a grave a little distance away from Imam Husain's. Perhaps in doing so he recalled that in life Habib Ibne Mazahir used to stand behind Imam Husain, with his arms folded and head reverentially bent. He imagined that even in death Habib might like to stand as a sentry near the grave of his Imam and beloved master. He had tried to shift the body of Abbas to the area where the other graves were prepared but he did not do so feeling some-what baffled as to why Imam Husain had left the body by the side of the river instead of brining it over to where the other bodies lay. He was sure that there must be some good reason for it, some real purpose behind it. He wondered whether Imam Husain had left the body of Abbas near the river to bring home same special association of his martyrdom with the flowing waters of the river. He even imagined that when he was thinking of disintering the body of Abbas for shifting it nearer to the graves of the other martyrs, the waters of the stream were raising a murmur of protest as if wanting him to be buried there as a reminder of some significant role his martyrdom had on the bank of the river. He then prepared Abbas's grave where he lay interred.

Jabir Ibn Abdullah Ansari had to scour a wide area to trace the graves of some of the martyrs. He found the bodies of Aun and Hur buried quite a distance away from the main field of battle. When he asked the men of Bani Asad tribe the reason for Hur being buried so far away from the battle-field, one of their elders replied that, as in case of all the other martyrs, Imam Husain had himself brought the body of Hur to the mortuary from the place where he had fallen and placed it there with his own hands. However, the old man told him, he had heard from some of the soldiers of Yazid's army that, when the battle was over and it was decided by Amr Ibn Saad, Commander of the forces of Yazid, that all the martyrs' bodies should be trampled under the hoofs of horses, the soldiers who were under the command of Hur had protested vehemently and, almost in a state of revolt, warned him that, if any action was taken to despoil or desecrate the body of Hur, they would, one and all, fight to the last. According to the old nun, this had deterred Amr Ibne Saad who fearing a mutiny in his army, had asked these rebellious soldiers of Hur's battalion to bury his corpse with full military honours. The soldiers who were under Hur's command had taken away his body for burial a good distance away so that even his grave could not be ravaged by the predators. Seeing this boldness on the part of Hur's soldiers in rescuing his dead body from depredation, many other soldiers, who had any relationship, even remote, with any of the followers of the Imam, came forward to claim the dead bodies of their relations so as to save them from being ravaged and trampled under the hoofs of the chargers. Even the hard-hearted Shimr had the brazen-facedness to say that, according to Arab custom, he would claim protection for the dead bodies of Abbas and his three brothers who were distantly related to him through their mother, lest he may incur the contempt of his contemporaries and colleagues for disregarding the ties of blood and not protecting the corpses of his blood relations.

When Jabir Ibn Abdullah heard this story, he wept bitterly asking whether there was not a soul amongst the hordes of Yazid on that day to say that Husein was the grandson, the most beloved child, of the Prophet, and he deserved their respect, if not in life, at least in death, on account of his ties of blood with the Prophet whom they claimed to revere as the last messenger of God! Could not any of them show respect for the relationship of Husain with the Prophet when they were vying with one another in saving the corpses of even their distant kitmred from despoiling!

****

Jabir Ibn Abdullah Ansari explained to his friends and companions that the reason why he had awakened them so early that morning was that in his dream he had seen the Holy Prophet who had told him that the captives' caravan, comprising Ali Zainal Abedeen, his infant son Muhammad al-Baqir, Husain's sisters Zainab and Umme Kulsum and other ladies of the Prophet's family were to reach Karbala that morning. The Prophet had asked him to go forward to greet them and to convey to them his

Salaams and condolences. He told his friends that he had awakened after this and he wanted them to accompany him so that they could go forward to receive the caravan and play hosts to the family of the Prophet.

By this time the first streak of dawn was visible on the eastern horizon. One of the entourage of Jabir recited the call to prayers and all of them offered their morning prayers and thanked Almighty Allah for giving them the opportunity of being not only the first pilgrims at the graves of the martyrs of Karbala, but also the first ones to greet the family of the Prophet on their return visit to the land, rendered sacred by the holy blood of the martyrs.

No sooner they had finished the prayers than they saw a cloud of dust rising in the distant horizon, indicating the approach of a caravan. Jabir and his friends rode their mounts to receive and welcome the Prophet's family. As soon as they were at a hailing distance, they got down from their steeds and, with profound respect, offered their salutations to Imam Ali Zainal Abedeen. Jabir Ibn Abdullah Ansari went over to the Imam and, holding the bridle of his horse, respectfully led him towards his camp on the banks of the river with the rest of the caravan following them. He told the Imam about the purpose of his visit to Karbla, what he had seen and heard during his halt there, and what he had done. He also respectfully enquired from Imam Ali Zainal Abedeen about the treatment meted out to him and the ladies of the Prophet's family. When this question was put to him, the Imam wept silently for quite some time and then softly replied: "O Jabir, it is a story of sufferings which will be written in blood and tears for future generations to read! What sufferings shall I recount to you which we endured after the great tragedy here? Our sufferings defy description."

When the ladies of Imam Husain's family saw the graves of their dear ones, they fell one by one from their camels, overcome by grief and sorrow. Each one rushed towards the grave of her son, brother, father or husband. Zainab darted straight towards the grave of Imam Husain, Umme Laila fell on the grave of Ali Akbar, Umme Farwa swooned on the tomb of Qasim and Umme Rabab clasped the tiny grave of her infant Ali Asghar. Umme Kulsum looked lost for a while as if she was searching for something and she hastened, after a little thought, towards the distant grave by the rivulet, where the flowing waters were singing a dirge on the martyrdom of her beloved brother Abbas. Each lady poured her heart over the grave of her dearest departed relarion, narrating all the sufferings she had endured. Zainab was heard to say on Imam Husain's grave: "My beloved brother, I have returned to you but without Sakina, whom you had, at the time of departing, entrusted to my care. My dearest brother, your beloved Sakina bore all the sufferings mutely and with fortitude till she could no longer endure them and surrendered her soul to her Maker. Forgive me, my dear brother, if i faltered in any way in fulfilling the mission you entrusted to me."

Imam Ali Zainal Abedeen watched silently for sometime the heart-rending scene, with tears streaming down his cheeks. When he saw that all the ladies had lightened their hearts, if that could ever be done, by recounting their woes and sufferings, he went over to each of them and persuaded them to leave the graves so that he, assisted by Jabir Ibn Abdullah Ansari and his friends, could bury the severed heads of the martyrs which he had brought with him all the way from Damascus. With a great deal of persuasion he succeeded in making the ladies do as he had requested. After washing the heads of the martyrs in the tributary of Euphrates he buried each head with the body to which it belonged. This task accomplished, he asked his aunt Zainab as to what she intended to do. She replied that, much as she would have liked to remain near the grave of her dearest brothers Husain and Abbas, her Ali Akbar, Ali Asghar, Qasim and her own sons, Aun and Muhammad, she remembered the parting wish of Imam Husain that she should return with the family to Medina. For her this wish was a command which she had to obey. Summoning up all her courage and controlling her overpowering feelings she made preparations to leave Karbala on the very next day to resume the homeward journey.

As on the 11th of Muharram in the fateful year 61 A.H., on this day also Zainab was performing the duty of assisting each lady of the house mount her camel. Much as the other ladies protested that it was almost sacriligious for them co let her perform this task, when they were there to help others and Zainab, she would not listen to them and insisted on performing this duty, saying that it was part of her mission to do what she had done once before, at this very place, after the carnage.

When all the ladies had mounted their camels, Zainab went over to see whether they were comfortable. She could not find Umme Rabab on her camel and so she started looking for her. She found her lying prostrate near the grave of her child Ali Asghar. Zainab went over to her and gently splashed water on her face to revive her. When she came to, she looked at Zainab and imploringly said;

"My lady, leave me to mv fate here so that I may die here and be buried by the graves of my child and my lord. What is there in Medina fro me to return to? My one beloved child I lost here and the other in Damascus. What does life hold for me after my losing all that I held dear in life and lived for?"

It required great efforts on Zainab's part to convince Umme Rabab that Imam Husain would have liked her to accompany the others to Medina. She at last succeeded and made her mount her camel. The caravan proceeded with Bashir Ibn Jazlam leading the procession, with a black banner in his hand and a black shawl round his neck to indicate that the mourners were bound on their homeward journey. Each lady was casting a longing, lingering look behind to see the graves of her beloved son, bother, nephew or husband under the baking sun of Nainevah.

****

The painfully slow journey of the captives of Karbala, like all mundane things, came to an end with their arrival in Medina on the 8th of Rabiul Awwal. With Bashir Ibn Jazlam singing the dirge of the martyrs sufferings to the accompaniment of moans and sobs of the bereaved family, the caravan entered the outskirts of Medina. Large throngs of people of Medina had come out to meet the family of the Prophet and offer them condolences. What a contrast it presented to the scene in Medina on the 28th of Rajab in the year 60 A.H. when these very same family had left Medina on their ill-fated journey! Few of the ladies on this day had any children in their arms or by their side. There were no youths riding beside them with airs of hope and confidence, beaming with vivacity, radiance and the joy of life. Instead the veiled faces of ladies bore deep marks of sorrow, wrinkles and furrows which depicted sufferings too deep for words, which no offering of condolences could alleviate, no expression of sympathy could mitigate.

Imam Ali Zainal Abedeen reverentially asked his aunt Zainab whether she wanted to go to her house with all the ladies to meet the large throng of sympathisers who were assembled there to condole the death of the martyrs. She, however, desired that she should first be taken to the tomb of the Prophet. Reaching the grave of the Prophet, she flung herself on it and, from a bundle which she was carrying, she took out the blood-stained garment of her brother which he was wearing at the time he was beheaded. She reverentially put it on the grave of her grandfather and, with one suppressed cry of anguish, she collapsed unconscious. The muffled cry she uttered expressed all the pent up emotions that were surging in her wounded and bleeding heart, much more than any words could have expressed.

The ladies of Bani Hashim, led by Ummul Baneen and Fatima Sugra had by now gathered round her and the other ladies of the Imam's family. They all did their best to revive her. When she came to, she thanked all those who were profusely offering her, and the other ladies, their sympathies and condolences and mourning over their sufferings. Supported by Ummul Baneen, mother of Abbas, and Fatima Sugra, she got up. She in her turn offered to Ummul Baneen her condolences on the death of her four brave sons in the defence of the Imam and the cause he stood for. She then picked up the blood stained shirt of Husain from the grave of the Prophet and, with faltering steps, walked over to the grave-yard nearby where lay buried her mother Fatima Zahra and her brother Imam Hasan Al-Mujtaba. When she reached her mother's grave, she put the blood soaked garment of Imam Husain on it and, falling on the grave and clasping it with both hands, she cried: "Mother, your Zainab has come, come alone to give you the tidings of your son's martyrdom, of the ruination of your house." She continued after a while: "O mother, how can I convey to you what indignities I have suffered, what insults I have endured, what brutalities I have been subjected to! Shall I show you the marks of the ropes that were tied so hard as to cut into my flesh?" Saying this she uncovered her hands where raw flesh was visible as a result of the cuts inflicted by the fetters tied on them during the days of her incarceration. She continued to moan: "O mother, do I have to show you what the tyrants' whips have done to our backs? Do I have to narrate to you what your beloved Husain and his sons and nephews and brothers, in the prime of their youth, suffered before their martyrdom? No, I know that you were with us in spirit during all our ordeals, even when my beloved Sakina used to cry with thirst or under the lashing of Shimr. You were there when we mourned and buried Sakina in her tiny grave in the prison of Damascus. My beloved mother, Zainab has fulfilled her appointed task by bringing back the captives' caravan to Medina. Now call me back to yourself, so that my weary body and soul may rest, may rest in peace which I have not known for a long, long time."

Zainab's recounting of sufferings and the outpouring of her heart, were bringing forth torrents of tears from the eyes of all who were near her on that day — much as their narration does even today, after more than 1300 years.

www.ingramcontent.com/pod-product-compliance
Lightning Source LLC
LaVergne TN
LVHW041927070526
838199LV00051BA/2739